Hip Santa Cruz 4

*First-person Accounts of
the Hip Culture of Santa Cruz
in the 1960s, 1970s, and 1980s*

*Edited by Ralph H. Abraham
with the assistance of
Rick Gladstone, Paul Lee,
Don Monkerud, and T. Mike Walker*

*Epigraph Books
Rhinebeck, New York*

Hip Santa Cruz 4. First person accounts of the Hip Culture of Santa Cruz, California in the 1960s, 1970s, and 1980s.

Copyright 2019 by Ralph H. Abraham. All rights reserved.

No part of this book may be used or reproduced in any manner without written permission from the publisher except in critical articles and reviews.

For information contact:
Epigraph Publishing Service
22 East Market Street, Suite 304
Rhinebeck, New York 12572
www.epigraphPS.com

Book Design by Deb Shayne.

ISBN 978-1-948796-53-8
Library of Congress Control Number: 2018964166

Bulk purchase discounts for educational or promotional purposes are available. Contact the publisher for more information.

CONTENTS

PREFACE	5
MEMORIAL GALLERY	9
CHRONOLOGY	11

Ch. 1. Futzie Nutzle
    I Had No Plan — 17
    Drawings — 29
Ch. 2. Dean Quarnstrom
    From Alpert to Ram Dass — 31
Ch. 3. Don Monkerud
    Mary Holmes — 38
Ch. 4. Jami Cassady
    The Barn Gave Me a Gift — 50
Ch. 5. Rick Alan
    Cathy Puccinelli Interview — 54
Ch. 6. Don Monkerud
    Scott Kennedy — 68
Ch. 7. Carmella Weintraub
    Saving the Soul of Santa Cruz — 83
Ch. 8. Ralph Abraham
    David Thiermann Interview — 95
Ch. 9. Rick Alan
    Out of the Haze — 107
Ch. 10. Mischa Adams
    I Picked It out of a Book — 118
Ch. 11. Frank Foreman
    21.1. Caffe Hip History — 136
    21.2. Drawings — 162
Ch. 12. Lynda Francis May
    4.1. Butterfly Productions — 166

Ch. 13. Don Monkerud	
Elizabeth Gips	*170*
Ch. 14. Ralph Abraham	
20.1. Nina Graboi	*180*
CONCLUSION	*183*
INDEX	*185*

PREFACE

In the 1960s, Santa Cruz was a fountainhead of Hip culture. When I arrived in 1968 to join the new university, UCSC, the creative time was nearly over. By 1980, it seemed to me it had been such a miracle that its birth should be recorded. So I created the Santa Cruz Hip History Project in 2002, collecting oral histories and photographs in a website:
http://www.ralph-abraham.org/1960s.

Original Concept, Volume #1.

The book *Hip Santa Cruz* published in June, 2016, was a compact summary of the 14 years accumulation of material from that website that was most relevant to the creation of the Hip culture of Santa Cruz. From 1964 to 1968, we followed the stories of some of the main characters of the Hip miracle in Santa Cruz, including 11 men and 2 women.

The book was presented to the Santa Cruz community in a reading and reunion at the Blitzer Gallery on August 6, 2016. Immediately there was a volunteering of additional stories, including several women, and stories into the 1970s. So I decided to create a sequel volume, *Hip Santa Cruz 2*.

New Concept, Volume #2.

In this second volume, I expanded the time-frame of the first volume, 1964-1968, up through the 1970s. My idea was to connect the decline of Hip culture with the ascent of the women's movement. Further, I wanted a balance of the genders consistent with the emerging equality of women and men, and here 50-50 was achieved. I ordered the chapters, as in the first volume, according to the approximate arrival date of the author in Santa Cruz.

In fact, the prime motive for this second volume was to balance the voices in the book according to gender, and to foreground the cultural transformation to Hip Women that occurred in the early 1970s.

New Concept, Volume #3.

The second volume was presented in a book launch event at the Santa Cruz Museum of Art and History on March 4, 2018. Once again there was a flood of offers of additional stories and interviews, so the idea of this third volume was born.

This time we again extended the time frame to follow the further evolution of the threads derived from the Hip Culture of the 1960s into the 1970s, and on into the 1980s. New threads have been included, such as music and the environmental movement. And several members of our community have stepped forward to assist me in the editing.

Concept, Volume #4.

This volume is a continuation of Volume #3.

Acknowledgements

I am very grateful to all the contributors and supporters of the Santa Cruz Hip History Project, and especially to my co-editors: Rick Gladstone, Kate Bowland, Paul Lee, Fred McPherson, Don Monkerud, Ed Penniman, and T. Mike Walker. Also I am deeply indebted to Becky Leuning for heroic typing of all the interviews, to Nada Miljkovic for two interviews she contributed to the second volume, and to Hiroko Tojo, Deb Shayne and Bruce Damer for logistic support.

Special Thanks

Special thanks to Paul Lee, my friend since my earliest days at UCSC, who has been an emotional support, and also partner in editing for content and typos, throughout this project. He and I are the only ones, up to now, who have repeatedly read every page of this book.

Finally, deep gratitude to Fred McPherson, also my friend since earliest days here, who has helped this project all along the way. Very sadly he passed away, just two days before this volume was completed.

— Ralph Abraham, Santa Cruz, November 10, 2018

Memorial Gallery

Mary Holmes, 1911-2002

Photo by Don Monkerud

Neal Cassady, 1926-1968

Photo thanks to Jami Cassady

CHRONOLOGY

Here is a brief chronology of some the main events of the time. To the items from the PREFACE of the preceding volume, *Hip Santa Cruz 2*, I have added a few new items, in bold, which are covered in the present text.

- 1930s, Swing bands in Capitola, Beach street (Ken)
- 1940s, Nine jazz clubs opened on Beach street (Ken)
- 1953, Willie Mae Thornton on Beach street (Ed)
- 1954, Two jazz clubs opened in Capitola (Ken)
- 1956, Rock & Roll banned in Santa Cruz (Rick)
- 1957, Dukes of R&R organised (Ed)
- 1958 --------
1. The Sticky Wicket, a cafe and gallery on Cathcart Street, was said to be the first Hip hangout. Later it moved to Aptos.
2. The Dukes of R&R formed (Rick Alan)
3. Bridge Mountain created (Holly Harmen)
4. Began teaching childbirth education (Celeste)
- 1959, Early years of Cabrillo (Roberta Bristol)
- 1960, Ken Kesey moved from the Wallace Stegner writing program at Stanford to La Honda and began house parties, along with LSD, fluorescent paintings, strobe lights, and music. Later, the house band became the Grateful Dead.
- 1961, Peter Demma, discharged from military service, moved to Palo Alto, met Ken Kesey and Neal Cassady
- 1962 --------
1. Leon Tabory, psychiatrist, moved into Neal Cassady's house in Los Gatos, and opened an office in Santa Cruz
2. Kesey published *One Flew Over the Cuckoo's Nest*
3. Santa Cruz chapter of the ACLU formed

4. Cabrillo moved to large campus (Roberta Bristol)
- 1963, Peter, while running a bookstore in San Diego, visited Big Sur. In the hot baths with Ron Bevirt a plan was hatched to open a bookstore in Santa Cruz called the Hip Pocket Bookstore. The sign was to be made by Ron Boise, a sculptor living in Big Sur in a bread truck. A set of his works called the Kama Sutra sculptures was then showing at the Sticky Wicket.
- 1964, Beginning of the golden years. --------
1. April 17, Site dedication of UCSC (Herb)
2. Ken Kesey published Sometimes a Great Notion, formed the Merry Pranksters. The bus Further took them to New York for a Kesey book event. Neal, Ron Bevirt, Lee Quarnstrom, Stewart Brand, Ed McClanahan, and others were on the trip.
3. Peter and Ron Bevirt opened the Hip Pocket Bookstore on September 13 in the St. George Hotel. The Ron Boise sign and two nude sculptures (covered by a sheet) were on hand. Norman Lezin, the mayor of Santa Cruz, had agreed to unveil the sculptures at the opening, which was busted by the police.
4. Later, Neal and Leon used to hang out and help out at the bookstore. Neal suggested the bookstore have free speech night every friday. Leon started them off, speaking about marijuana.
5. Leon hears Eric "Big Daddy" Nord was opening the Loft, a cafe at a barn in Scotts Valley. Leon went there, met Cathy, they married.
- 1965 -----
1. November 21, Wavy Gravy's Lysergic A GO GO in LA, with light show by Del Close. (See www.rollingstone.com/music/news/acid-tests-turn-50-wavy-gravy-merry-prankster-ken-babbs-look-back-20151130.)

2. November 27, the first Acid Test, in Soquel, near Santa Cruz.
3. UCSC opened in the Fall.
4. The Hip Pocket Bookstore closed. Ron Lau purchased the books.

- 1966 --------
1. Bookshop Santa Cruz opened by Ron Lau
2. In the summer, the Barn opened in Scotts Valley by Leon. It featured dances similar to the acid tests, with fluorescent wall paintings by Joe Lysowski and Pat Bisconti. Great artists such as Janis Joplin and Country Joe performed there. A local band performed on musical sculptures created by Ron Boise. Light shows created by Joe were among the first in the US.
3. Paul Lee (philosopher, founding editor of The Psychedelic Review) joined UCSC
4. In the Fall, the Catalyst Coffee House and Delicatessen, run by Al And Patti DiLudovico, opened in the St. George Hotel next to the Bookshop.
5. Trips Festival in San Francisco (Paula)
6. The Jefferson Airplane played a benefit for the "Miller for Congress" campaign at the Civic Auditorium (Rick)

- 1967 --------
1. Jefferson Airplane played in Santa Cruz.
2. Hippies moved into the Holiday Cabins in Ben Lomond. (See Holly Harman, *Inside a Hippie Commune*, 2015, for the full story.)
3. 1000 Alba Road community created by Raven Lang and Ken Kinzie
4. Methuselah I, summer camp at UCSC
5. Alan Chadwick arrives at UCSC
6. Start of the Chadwick Garden (Paul)
7. Summer, the *Redwood Ripsaw* (started by Tom

Scribner, Rick Gladstone, John Tuck, John Sanchez, Carol Staudacher — and Paul Lee was also at the first organizational meeting) began publication. It was the first "alternative press" published in Santa Cruz (Rick).
8. **Monterey Pop Festival (Nutzle)**
9. **Balloon Newspaper formed (Nutzle)**
10. **Scott Kennedy comes to UCSC (Scott)**
- 1968 -----
1. Spring, I visited UCSC and the Barn, and decided to join UCSC (Ralph)
2. Fall, I arrived with family. Moved into a 24-room Victorian mansion at 724 California Street.
3. Fall, The Kite (cafe) opened at UCSC
4. **Woodstock Festival (Carmela, Nina)**
- 1969 -----
1. The Barn closed
2. The Catalyst closed
3. Jack Kerouac died
4. I got into trouble at UCSC for political actions, along with Paul Lee.
5. Odyssey Records opened (Rich Bullock) with the Occult Shop (Lew Fein).
6. Logos Books and Records opened (John Livingston).
7. Fritjof Capra's epiphany.
8. November, the *Free Spaghetti Dinner*, the original local alternative newspaper to which all subsequent alternative weeklies can trace their roots, began publication at the Blaine Street Family Collective (Rick)
9. **Altamont (Nutzle)**
10. **Pot farming began in Santa Cruz (Rick)**
- 1970, The end of the golden years --------
1. February 26. In the local alternative newspaper, *The Free Spaghetti Dinner*, I wrote in my regular column

"Scientific Advice on the Politics of Life," under my pseudonym, Dr. Abraham Clearquill: "Last Fall I felt that the emerging community in Santa Cruz was at a watershed, and that a development of some importance to the world was possible. Now I am convinced that this opportunity has passed, and the old structure is being recreated." (Thanks to Rick Gladstone, founding editor of the FSD, for recalling this.)(Ralph)
2. June, we vacated the Victorian mansion (Ralph)
3. The decline of Hip, and ascent of the Women's Movement.
4. Santa Cruz Birth Center started (Raven Lang)
5. Warmth created by Don McCaslin (T. Mike)
6. First ecology course at UCSC (Fred)
7. Oganookie arrived in Brookdale (Jack)
8. Fall, Krishna Cafe opened (Ralph)
9. Jazz instruction began at Cabrillo (Ken)
10. Start of the USA (Paul)
11. Start of the Whole Earth Restaurant (Herb)

- 1971 --------
1. Women's dances began in San Lorenzo valley
2. Oganookie first appearance, UCSC (Jack)
3. Community on Last Chance Road (Paula)
4. Raven started the Birth Center (Celeste)

- 1972 --------
1. Beginning of action to stop SLV development (Fred)
2. The Birth Book published (Celeste}
3. Tandy Beal came to Cabrillo (Roberta Phillips)
4. Don McCaslin began Warmth (Ken)
5. Start of the William James Association (Paul)

- 1973 --------
1. Save the San Lorenzo Valley Association formed (Fred)
2. Oganookie ended (Jack)

3. Construction of Caffe Pergolesi (Frank)
- 1974 --------
1. SC Birth Center busted (Kate Bowland)
2. Emergence of the Hanuman Foundation (Roberta McPherson)
3. Nurse Midwife Practice Act passed
4. Hanuman Tape Library formed (Paula)
5. **Wilder Ranch saved (Carmela)**
6. **Good Fruit Company opened (David)**
- 1975, Theater program began at Cabrillo (Ken)
- 1976 -----
- 1. Start California Conservation Corps (Paul)
- **2. Resource Center for Nonviolence formed (Scott)**
- 1977 -----
1. Kuumbwa opened (Ken)
2. **LSD Colloquium I at UCSC (Lynda)**
- 1978 -----
1. Institute of Feminine Arts created (Raven Lang)
2. Mount Madonna opened (Paula)
3. Start of the Valley Women's Club (Nancy)
4. **Pogonip saved (Carmela)**
5. **Lighthouse Point saved (Carmela)**
- 1981 -----
1. **LSD Colloquium II at UCSC (Lynda)**
2. **Beginning of Butterfly Productions (Lynda)**

Chapter 1: Futzie Nutzle (AKA: Bruce Kleinsmith)
I Had No Plan....
T. Mike Walker, Ed.

I was born in 1942 and grew up in the blue-collar town of Fostoria, Ohio, 100 miles from Cleveland. My father died after being wounded three or more times in the Battle of the Bulge during the final days of the Second World War.

My step-father was Irish, a tough decorated veteran of the Army Air Force who could be very intimidating. I was sixteen at the time and started driving a dump truck, shoveling iron and sand, melting iron for my step-father's new recycling business. And I have to say as an artist, it was beautiful — except for the part of getting inside the smokestack and relining it with brick and clay for the next firing; very claustrophobic. I hated that. We'd take the iron that had been dumped by the Auto-Lite foundry next door and put it in this smokestack and melt it, and then the slag and everything would go off on one end and I would tap a hole of clay, and pure white iron would shoot out into black sand grooves that I'd made on the ground with a shovel. They would turn orange, and then red, and then lead-color and I'd break it up with a sledgehammer and throw the bars on the truck. That was my job. But those colors, especially at sundown — I mean, I had to watch where I stepped or I'd burn my foot off! It was fantastic, and I didn't mind the labor. The aesthetic of that was better than any Hopper painting — it was real!

As far as Charles Henry (my step-dad and boss) was concerned, no one in the world was more honest or hard working. But it was a disaster trying to work with used machinery, and during the recession of 1958 we went down — along with the iron prices dropping to a trickle.

My mother never got over the loss of my dad. She was

very artistic with a great sense of aesthetic, humor and style. She worked at John B. Rogers Costume Company, and as a millenary specializing in hats. I inherited her ability to draw or render; she really had a special personal touch; her drawings were beautiful.

When I finished High School in 1960, I had no plan, but cartooning was high on my list. My friend John and I headed west for Balboa Island in his red MG, Route 66 style, looking for a new sense of freedom. After a great trip across country with countless adventures, I returned to Ohio and my job back at the foundry loading slag steel and driving the "Diamond T" dump truck at my stepdad's recycling business, looking for traction of some sort to move on. I got a job as a house appraiser — measuring, drawing floor plans with my 10 ft. pole, checking the interior of every dwelling and looking for illegal rooms, etc. It was a hideous job, seeing the spectrum of the rich and poor and how they chose to live. I preferred the foundry. This was the very beginning of conscious observations.

At the end of summer I enrolled at Ohio State and started cartooning for Sundial, the humor magazine distributed throughout the college campuses across the nation. Phil Ochs was our editor, who was very encouraging, giving me page after page of space and even a cover for the holiday season's edition. I think it was 1961.

I didn't figure on social gathering as important events; I shunned meetings, fraternity rushes, ROTC and other clubs. A columnist for the Review Times in my hometown connected me with Milton Caniff, one of the premier cartoonists of America, author of Steve Canyon and Terry and the Pirates. I ignored his advice — studies of economics and politics, including my participation in the ROTC Air Force maneuvers. Anticipating a new thrust in cartooning and not wanting to work for a syndicate, I also began to realize that as a cartoonist, observations could be as important as activism.

Somehow, I got a job with DARE magazine in Cleveland, a conservative rag with a few liberal ideas. I wanted to base my work on personal humor, beginning with cartoon panels and punch lines — complex weak attempt with little direction. After five quarters, I moved to Cleveland and started working for Federman, Adams and Colopy, an advertising agency with highbrow clients like Bonnie Bell Cosmetics and General Motors. As an apprentice, I also attended the Cooper School of Art and the Cleveland Art Institute. None of this activity stuck. It was a miserable winter in Cleveland, grim and nowhere; so I headed to Ft. Lauderdale in my 1951 Cadillac Hearse and a new job at the Bahama Hotel.

I was living with some like-minded friends, serving continental breakfasts at the Bahama. But I was fired for parking my hearse too close to the hotel. My life became a cloud of circumstances. I ended up living in a garden shed, spending my days raking weeds from a fishpond, generally heading towards a mental collapse. I finally left Florida and headed back to Ohio, trying to sell my hearse to funeral homes in poor rural neighborhoods along the way.

By the next summer I still thought of cartooning, with Ronald Searle being an influence, along with the "new" style of cartooning called "Black Humor." Magazines like Mad, Trump, Cracked, etc. changed the idea of cartooning, and I was still on the tourist wheel of jobs, heading once again for fame and fortune in my 56 Sedan deVille. I found a job in South Lake Tahoe at Barney's Casino. After a month or two of PJ sandwiches and tubs of alcohol saturation and mindless nights of working in the coin room, my pal RG and I left and drove West to the Bay Area.

Let me back up for a minute. In 1961 I was still at Ohio

State University, unable to grasp anything of value. I shared a small house with "Short Arms," my mathematician room mate, before getting another place with Snidely Whiplash from Lima, Ohio. I met Snidely in one of the first Art classes, a Drawing class taught by John Hunter, who had lived in Southern California. The first day of his class, he came into the classroom with "News From the Colosseum: The latest scores — Lions 4, Christians Nothing!" I was on the floor laughing — I mean it was 1961 and this was happening to me? I couldn't figure it out...then he pointed in my direction and asked me to step out into the hallway.

"Oh Jeez" I thought. John then invited me to spaghetti dinner that evening at his house in Columbus. We were instant friends, and as I write this we still are. Man oh man, could he draw!

Meanwhile, back in 1965, leaving Tahoe on a rather sour note, I remembered my old teacher and pal from OSU. John had just returned from Italy after receiving a Fulbright and we were headed to San Jose and Hunter's studio, hoping for a place to cool out. Snidely headed to San Francisco where he rented a place on Kearny behind Finocchio's. I stayed with John right away in his Eichler home studio and kept hearing about Santa Cruz. I pictured adobes by the sea and talked RG into driving over the hill on Highway 17 to have a look-see.

That's when we decided to make a go of it on a foggy cool Fall day in 1965. We rented a cottage across the river from the Boardwalk for $80 a month. He sold insurance and I scouted for antiques, with the limited knowledge I had learned while in Columbus. I liked the antique dealers in Santa Cruz who gave me tinsel-tart jobs, enough to keep me afloat, I loved it! I liked everyone. Assimilating into Santa Cruz was easy for me. I liked the antique dealers, the decorators, the surfers, the artists, musicians, poets, and the no-accounts. I opened my own hole-in-the-wall antique junk store across from Orange Julius and Otto's Surf Rental. I also took a space at Village Fair in Aptos, while painting a sign for Rags and Riches. We made crab nets from old lampshades and fished off the wharf a short distance from our cottage on the cliff.

My paintings were cartoony, but I did them anyway, getting my first show in Santa Cruz in June of 1966. Monk D'Anna owned Monk's across from the Boardwalk's Penny arcade on the corner. I also had a few things at the Chamberlin Galleries on 325 Ocean. I enjoyed hanging out at Monk's as he had a turntable and played Jazz records, changing the shows every two months. A painting was stolen and I finally took Mr. D'Anna to court, but I lost my case, even though I had a witness for a verbal contract of theft. So much for 1966.

We moved from the cottage to Hubbard Gulch Rd. in Ben Lomond. The Wagon Wheel Bar was my new hangout until I was thrown out because of my lack of a haircut. I still kept painting. The cabin was quiet and perfect for studio work, while listening to KFRC AM. After a night of beer drinking at Monk's, I flopped at a friend's shop only to be awakened by a knock on the door. A woman from Saratoga was looking for oval picture frames and I happened to have a few at the cabin. She was looking for antiques, so I suggested Walter Mole in Los Gatos. He had a special sense of Art, unusual objects, and scale, so we went there. Mole offered me the empty rooms upstairs, a perfect studio, and his gallery for a show. My work fit in pretty well amongst the big guns from Stanford, SJ State and other schools and galleries. So I had a studio, a gallery, room for a few friends, and the good life.

Somehow I heard about a new club called Wayne Manor, after Batman's Mansion, in Sunnyvale. I went there. Joe Lysowski was painting the interior, and he introduced me to everyone around the club. The owners were very hip:

Susie Cream-cheese, the boutiques and wack jobs. Lysowski had stuff going on everywhere. Our synchronicity was phenomenal. I remember an example of this: I was driving with my girlfriend to Needles, hoping to find a place to swim in the Colorado. We pulled into a place by the river and there was Lysowski and family hanging out near Ron Boise's bread truck. He talked us into following him and Wendy and their son Shaun up to Oatman, Arizona, where the Hell's Angels were hiding out. We stayed in Oatman a week or so, going to potlucks and basically just hanging out. I mention our synchronicity because a couple of years later he came by and the two of us took Boise's Thunder Machine to Altamont, in December of 1969. We parked the flatbed 20 or so yards from stage right and nodded off, sleeping in the cab. By the next day, just as the music started, the truck and the Thunder Machine were covered with people from Santa Cruz. How we were spotted in that sea of concert goers is anyone's guess. There was violence happening right in front of us..the man in the chartreuse suit, the Hells Angels, the Stones; it became a surreal drama with a lot of us wishing it was over. Joe and I went back to Santa Cruz, returning the Thunder Machine, but I was still in minor shock, not remembering our return or what we did with Boise's sculpture. After that I lost interest in mega-concerts, even though I loved the music.

    Speaking of music, Thursday nights were reserved for 25th Century Ensemble sessions. Max Hartstein opened his studio by the river in Ben Lomond for anyone who wished to be included in the music. He asked me to design his idea of an image that would serve as the perfect logo for the ensemble, finally settling on a flying lion. I drew the image in pen and ink, placing the lion on a burning sphere inside a traditional oval format. He was pleased with the image, realizing we could work together on future projects, notably the art for one of our best compositions, "Indian Dogman".

Back home, I continued painting and making art for the Walter Mole Gallery. Mole kept mentioning another artist, Victor Harlow. I finally went to his studio. Whoa! He showed me his drawings and a few paintings that gave me a whole new way of appreciation and improvisation. The rendering was there, plus humor, sophisticated line, and ideas. Seemingly crude at first, but oh! — a nut grabber. Victor was about to move, looking at Santa Cruz for a place to recuperate after major surgery. So I volunteered to help him, not knowing what might be in store for me. My decision proved to be a fantastic choice. His dad rented us a trailer and cabana on Larch Lane at Pleasure Point in — you guessed it — Santa Cruz.

We met and hung with a whole "new" bunch of creatives. At night we'd sit across from each other at a table listening to jazz while working on our "Sick and Well" series of cartoons in a challenging manner. By the end of 1966 we were plugged in. Surfers, artists, and old friends from Ohio stopped in. Weed seeped in somehow. There was so much: shopping bags full, lining the walls. Rolling bombers or fatties became a full time job. We weren't outlaws, but rather escapees from academia. The people that I knew didn't consider weed a party drug. In the '60's, especially on the West Coast, most thought of weed and LSD as important tools for augmenting consciousness.

Once again synchronicity was on my side. I met Lysowski, coincidently, on the cliff at Pleasure Point and he told me about his friends the Pranksters. He kept mentioning them, and one day there they were in our driveway. Neal at the wheel. I boarded the Further Bus, had a tuna sandwich prepared on board, and headed to LA. Victor jumped aboard at the last second for the ride of a lifetime. Watching Neal drive was unbelievable. With a bomber in his left hand, a girlfriend on his knee, a can of beer, his right hand free, somehow, for the gearshift and steering wheel. We were on our way with loudspeakers blasting overtures and other sounds. I could see that Neil could see everything, every pebble on the highway. Another bus, with a tie-dye interior and hooka, followed us with laughing gas fresh from Dominican Hospital.

LA was a whole new reality. I popped out unscathed. Almost. My first experience on LSD, with a loving guide, gave me a new view of everything. I became a different person, deciding to design my life, instead of living randomly. It started to work, but not in LA. I went back to a fresh Lilly-pad in Santa Cruz and began a new approach to painting and drawing, leaning towards different thinking and execution.

1967 looked promising. Victor and I exhibited our new attempts at humor, including his pile of rags at Cupola Gallery near Twin Lakes. We ruffled feathers but not intentionally. No, there was no acid in the punch, although a lot of folks thought there must be, staring at the pile of rags and trying to interpret my "Bea and Stan don't live here anymore" construction. We topped off the evening by escaping in a Rolls Royce furnished and driven by a furrier from San Jose. He was so patient waiting at the back door with us running out, chased by our friends, hopping into the Rolls and leaving it all behind. Max Hartstein filmed the whole thing from up above on a roof or balcony in 16mm. Nothing really happened, but it seemed like it! We closed early, gearing up for the following day — the Monterey Pop Festival. We asked friends to watch the gallery, but we got the boot instead.

We went to Monterey and built a cheesy gallery of plywood and gesso. Our work stood out. There were no references of weed, tie-die or hip influence in our display. People looked in and merrily went on their way. Just as the Sunday night was warming up, a woman handed me a ticket for one of the most famous concerts ever! Monterey changed everything once again.

I'm a little hazy on the chronology after that 1967 Summer, but soon Henry Humble joined us in forming The Balloon Newspaper in an old Turkey Shed across from Dominican Hospital. The Balloon was a cartoon newspaper with no news and improvisation-ally foolish, crude humor, always a guest artist, with some solid panels, quips and a vehicle for distribution of our cartoons through the mail. We carried on, evolving our work and moreover, it was damn fun! I think Pat Bisconti was our first guest artist, and I began working on the illustrations for his Da Da Duck storybook. I remember too, hanging out during the lunch hour at Ralph Abraham's.

Meanwhile, back at The Balloon, Victor became Spinny Walker, Phil Sievert, my friend from Cooper School, chose henry humble. and I chose Futzie Nutzle for a variety of reasons. I felt the future would be a rough road for cartooning and I needed a fresh approach. I was getting published under my real name, Bruce Kleinsmith, and showing here and there with professional people, but something was gnawing at me. The art world was so unbelievably crazy and phony, I couldn't deal with it from a realistic point of view at that time, because it just looked like it was this big ball of hair that was gonna be trouble. So Futzie Nutzle seemed perfect. The Z's stood out on the printed page; the name was meaningless, yet phonetic. Finally, Richard Meynell came out of nowhere, finding us after seeing a poster I had done for the Universal Unitarian Church on Freedom Boulevard. He grew up on the East Coast, spending hours on Park Avenue and in the museums in Manhattan. He was convinced that we were on the cutting edge of a new movement. He became our scribe: A. Blinken.

The thing I lacked was a style, but by 1970 I cornered a style of drawing, practicing, and a process of elimination. While others were going psychedelic, I wanted a distinctive, simple, fine ink line, set off against a stark white background for minimalist clarity. Cartooning for the markets became more and more complex, but we wanted simplicity, art with teeth, captioned and riddle-like, working towards a certain quality. We broke through on several levels, creating mild interest in town, creating miles of art. We began submitting cartoons to all the local rags, created billboard art and hooked up with the NY Correspondence school and artists from San Francisco, and Image Bank in Vancouver. A few followers and friends supported us, including Frank and Carol DePalma of the Harbor Cafe on 7th Ave., donating their time and a bus that hauled us to events, including the 2nd Joint Show, featuring SF's poster artists and the 25th Century Ensemble... Dave and Jon Sievert, humble's brothers, shot pictures of us so we had documentation.

It was a community of thinkers, scholars, independent writers and artists. Music can't be left out because it was happening everywhere including anyone who wanted to participate. Somehow it was all interconnected. Everyone knew someone from every source. It is impossible to write a real, concise history of that time — there was a general acceptance of people's directions all fitting together like tongue and groove; respect wasn't spoken, but it was there. Balloon evolved and so did we. The three of us devised "The Combo Drawings...", all of us drawing on a large sheet of paper at the same time, improvising on a selected theme submitted beforehand, based on the principle of making each other laugh! We had a PO Box 2481 at the Seabright Post Office. Martin Blakemore, postal worker at the window, was always positive, had a laugh every time we opened our box or mailed objects never before sent in the US mail — such as a pair of oars, shipped separate and unwrapped with a tag on each one.

We moved again, this time to Mission Street near Walnut in an old Victorian formally rented by an artist named Don Chamblis. Zarko and his family of gypsies came by often to play their music and dance in our kitchen. Meanwhile, humble and I started a mural covering the west wall of the The White Buffalo. We met Rita Bottoms of Special Collections at UCSC, then Neal Coonerty of Bookshop SC and Frank Foreman at Cafe Pergolesi. We were surprised that Rita was so supportive, and Neal helped me by introducing me to Thames and Hudson, who published my first book of cartoons entitled Modern Loafer, in 1980.

All of this led to our show at the Santa Cruz Library with the courage and blessing from Charles Atkins. The Balloon had arrived! On a Friday night we opened S.C.A.M.P. (Santa Cruz Artists Media Project), a gallery on the corner of Soquel and Pacific, on April 13th, 1974. There were five or six of us, including P. Hefferton, C. Prentiss, D. Weaver, D. Sievert, humble, Spinny, me and many great people who had a similar ideal of an open gallery for anyone who fit in. I think Silver Chalice was the band, and it was horrible. I soon realized I needed to get back to my goal: drawing. Santa Cruz art seemed caught between academia and professionalism. I needed a job,

Due to a fluke and timing, along with an introduction, I landed my own column on the Letter's Page in Rolling Stone Magazine from 1975-1980. A bi-monthly, I needed to come up with something that would fit, something simple, semi-topical, musical or whatever. My style began to emerge, getting simpler and simpler, but still with juice. By 1978 I had it nailed — at least I thought so. I continued cartooning for Free Spaghetti Dinner, The Independent, Rags, The Leviathan, Boston's Real Paper, Rolling Stone, Metro, Sacramento Review, Sundaz, the Bay Guardian, the Japan Times in Tokyo, Wet and

File, as well as other publications.

Ah, Santa Cruz! The merchants knew the students, the students knew the surfers, the surfers knew the artists and hippies, and the hippies knew the politicians and the politicians knew everyone, all of them claiming to be liberal!

I honestly thought writing this sketch would be pretty easy. I was naïve about that. I kept most of the photos, papers, correspondence, etc. from 1967 to 1977. Everyone was busy living two lives: the life they had before Santa Cruz, and the life they designed after moving here.

Always a fresh palette! Santa Cruz is, as ever, dominated by the beauty of Monterey Bay and a seashore of freedom.

Chapter 2: Dean Quarnstrom
From Alpert to Ram Dass

I had a source for pure LSD from a new friend, Richard Alpert, a former Harvard professor who'd just moved from Boston/New York to California to teach at Stanford. Manny and I returned to our Homer Lane cottage from a road trip to Mexico City and back; our unlocked front door opened to an amazingly different living-room, in fact a new and unfamiliar world than the sparsely furnished-cum-crash pad cabin we'd left only two weeks before. Our friendly next-door neighbor had offered her East Coast friend, Richard Alpert, the use of the cottage while we were away.

Alpert had moved himself right in, completely re-decorating the entire interior with oriental rugs, Tibetan Tongkas, enlarged photo posters of mystics and spiritual leaders, including a six-foot poster close-up of Meher Baba's serenely happy-face, plus a variety of the latest swirling, eye-dazzling psychedelic posters. Gauzy rainbow-colored Indian-print bedspreads floated gracefully overhead, billowing in the refreshing afternoon breeze pouring in through an open window, covering the no-nonsense bland plaster ceiling. Large pillows were scattered around on the room-sized Oriental rug, and not a proper chair in sight; Sai Baba's powerful incense, Nag Champa, along with soft Indian raga background music, filled my senses.

A smiling 30's-something stranger was relaxing, spread across a few pillows, his balding scalp barely hidden by a thinning clump of dark hair pulled into a classic comb-over; his protruding, gumball-sized eyes seemed to float out from deep-set eye sockets, shaded by an enormous, protruding forehead. He introduced himself with a warm, "Hello, you must be Dean and Manny. I'm Richard. Jane said I could crash here if I took care of Howard, (my cat). Hey, I'm just about to drop some really good Acid, would you care to join in, take a trip?" I felt like I'd known the man forever.

This was the very same Richard Alpert that I'd heard and read so much about, a psychologist and renowned expert on psychedelic drugs. Newspaper reports claimed he'd turned-on Boston, Harvard and the East Coast. I owned a copy of his book "The Tibetan Book of the Dead," which I'd kept close at hand during my first LSD trip. Wow! This was far out, he'd moved in, he's here, living in my house!

Without missing a beat, Manny and I both accepted his offer, "It'd be a real pleasure, it's great to finally meet you, too."

I popped the sugar cube into my mouth that Alpert offered, then he put a cube on his own tongue, Manny followed suit and off we went.

Our trip lasted for 48 hours, what with we all refueling with more cubes along the way. We travelled through a universe of places and spaces we'd each discovered and freely shared, both with and without spoken words, within one another's minds and dreams, fears and passions, a consciousness shared within the safety of this soft, peaceful environment. We each told stories from our lives, both spoken and without words; psychic interactions that I'd believed were impossible to feel and share freely with another human, another man, and especially with a gay man, as Richard revealed without fear or shame to anyone. No secrets were withheld, intimate personal stories flowed from a fountain of knowledge within each of us, deep and powerful truths, simultaneously felt and understood by one another.

What passed between us was god-like, real communication without words; even the few moments of personal stress, fears, were handled so gently by our experienced guide and new friend, a fearless explorer of the consciousness of inner space. We traveled through forms of realities beyond the senses; truths about existence were revealed and shared, and this knowledge, in turn, opened my heart and soul to the grand potential, hidden deep-within every form of life. Every question was answered, no truth illuminated was left unexplored, and we, ever so softly, gently, revealed to one another our most-secret, darkest fears, which, for reasons rendered meaningless, had been hidden away from conscious awareness.

Richard and I developed a bond of friendship, of mutual trust and acceptance, and a deep love that's lasted our lifetimes. The experience was a major lesson for me on friendship and trust that transcended our genders and sexual identities. Richard, who later changed his name to Ram Dass, remains a close friend today, over 50 short years later. Now, as I look back, I have to ask myself, how often in one's life does one make a friendship such as this, one that lasts forever? Rarely to never.

Richard asked me to work with him; he needed help arranging a series of lectures throughout the country on LSD and the spiritual experience that this mind-altering substance made available to man.

Perfect, Richard! Yes, I'd love to work with you, in fact, it's exactly what I'd like to be doing right now, I responded.

As I wanted a place of my own to live, and I still was exploring this new San Francisco Bay Area world of free-thinking people, I naturally moved on to the next great frontier of cultural experimentation, Berkeley, to explore and to exploit, and rented a secluded, rustic cabin hidden behind a larger Victorian on Chandler Way and close to the university. So, on to Berkeley it was, on to it's abundance of young women looking to discover the possibilities of living and being free. I began arranging lecture events along the

West Coast for the rising cultural hero, Richard Alpert, who was spreading the good word about LSD from Canada to the beaches of Southern California. Things were turning out well; I continued this work, and continued to explore my inner self with Acid as often as I could.

Richard mentioned that, at the same time I was setting up his lectures, and only if I was comfortable doing so, I could make some serious money for both of us by distributing his pure LSD to a few trusted people he knew in the cities I'd be visiting; he'd supply the LSD to me along the way.

Alpert, and his ex-partner at Harvard, Tim Leary, had become the public faces in the media supporting the "dangerous, illegal psychoactive drug, LSD" and Richard couldn't risk distributing it himself in the US after its recent government classification as an illegal Class 1 substance, in the same category as heroin. But the 60's Generation felt differently about its use and importance for mankind, and I was up for the offer and the income.

Taking a road trip with Alpert, now we're talking 'bout some real fun! The bottom line gist of this gig was that I would start on the West Coast, rent a large auditorium or hall in major cities, place announcements in the local papers, and seed these markets with high-quality acid a few weeks before Alpert's speaking event, creating a new demand for acid as well as an opportunity; for the price of a lecture ticket, one could learn straight from the expert about what they'd recently experienced while taking the LSD. Bottom line, we might help heal those few whose minds were completely blown-out by the acid trip, and also earn some good cash income. "Hey, out there, anyone listening..? I need a little help over here! I think I've lost my mind…"

For the price of admission to his lectures. Richard would offer advice and give information to everyone who needed or wanted to know what had just happened to them, to all these new customers of ours after taking this substance. I'd often deliver bottles of aspirin with 250 mcg of LSD dropped onto each pill: my motto, "cures headaches two ways."

The plan worked, creating large audiences in every city we visited for Alpert's lectures on Psychedelics, building the attendances for each new lecture meant greater income from ticket sales for "An Evening with Richard Alpert" lecture. The events were similar to today's social networking events, large gatherings of similarly-minded, curious people in each city who shared the LSD experience as their reason to attend. The LSD lecturing was happening at the same time that Kesey's Merry Pranksters were on the road performing their own promotions for LSD and it's mind-altering experiences; The Acid Test "Happenings" were being held throughout California.

Create a demand for Acid, then fill it, and, if a few souls were driven outta their minds, hey, don't worry too much; someone will be dropping by real soon, maybe spend an evening explaining to all the lost souls how to find themselves again. This is what Alpert did best.

Pure genius, I said to myself. I mean, there were no guidebooks or ground rules yet established for exploring the mind's inner-spaces, and the 60's people were interested enough and willing to pay a small fee to learn more about their recent experiences.

I'd rent a 2000 seat auditoriums in Berkeley, or Vancouver, Santa Monica, Seattle, place advertising in local bookstores and in local newspapers, set up radio interviews on the newly-hip underground FM radio stations, and sell quantities of pure LSD in each city Alpert would be speaking. When Richard showed up a month later, there were always a few unfortunates still suffering from their encounter with the psychedelic, the

Acid Casualties, those very few who hadn't "Passed the Acid Test," waiting in line the night of the event, desperate to finally understand what had happened. With my LSD supplier's blessing, and a few trusted contacts in the important cities, I expanded, hit the road early in 1965, spreading this seed of change across the land, and, in my own small way, helping fuel the 60's Revolution.

I was welcomed graciously everywhere I travelled, and delivered quantities of LSD to Seattle, to Portland, San Diego, Laguna Beach and Santa Barbara; I received an enthusiastic welcome in Chicago, selling "the good shit" to new friends and then to their friends, who spread it through Old Town, the Near North, Evanston's Northwestern U., and the U of Chicago's beatnik/hipster students, and outwards from there, in all directions. They were lined up and waiting for acid in Ann Arbor and in Akron, Ohio. New Yorkers welcomed me as well, although not being the first to deliver Acid to the East Village crowd; no matter, they sure did love the pure product I brought to them, and they'd take as much of Owsley's finest, his infamous "White Lightning," as I could bring as well.

Every city provided a new magical adventure for me, each with its own variety of hip, underground culture to explore, understand, embrace, and try to appreciate despite disparities between one city to the next. In Chicago, my new "Best Friend," George, was so excited that I'd actually showed up with the pure Acid that he had no alternative but to reciprocate with an equal, and to him, a "Best of Chicago" gesture. He produced from the depths of his dark, Navy Pea-coat, and presented to me a cherished possession, his chrome-plated,. 38 Colt Police Special pistol, said he'd personally stolen it from a Chicago cop. "A real beauty, don'cha think, bud," he said, grinning from ear to ear, "take it, it's yours."

"Real groovy, man….ah, George, it's great." I'd met George

at Big John's, on North Wells Street, where The Butterfield Blues Band was performing, and we were standing in plain sight along the side wall, Having grown up amongst this city's love of handguns, I wasn't freaked out by the sight of a pistol, but I'd left this cool, tough-guy life and attitude behind when I'd moved to the Bay Area, and without regret. I asked George, "Uh, dude, think maybe you could, uh, mail it to me?"

This powerful, mind-altering new drug turned many business encounters into other exciting opportunities for new sexual encounters. It was a total gas to open new, hip markets with a great product, providing a well-paid service for appreciative customers; Johnny Appleseed was rewarded on every level, in every part of the country. I didn't consider, or treat this offered respect with the same attitude as many rock musicians treated their new groupies, as purely sexual encounters to be expected, but I didn't shy away from sexual invitations when the vibes were right. I was good at handling bulk sales, I was careful, honest and not afraid to face and take risks, and quickly gained the trust and recognition of my suppliers. I was creating my own success.

Later, after Richard had spent a year travelling, and then sitting at the feet of his new guru, Neem Karoli Baba, in India, then moved back to his family house in New Hampshire finishing his book, Be Here Now,, and a stint with fellow spiritual seekers in Taos, New Mexico, where he published this book, my good friend, now-known-as Ram Dass, moved into the house I'd acquired in Soquel, CA, and next door to my home, we again picked up our relationship and I became his official Tour Manager for a coming speaking tour, this time promoting the wonders of his recent journey discovering and living a spiritual life.

Chapter 3: Don Monkerud
Mary Holmes — Always Ready to Speak Up for Art:

Like Japan, which honors its outstanding artists, craftsman and teachers as living treasures, Santa Cruz too has extraordinary teachers and artists who we revere and respect. Approaching 90 years old, Mary Holmes certainly falls into that category. Both a painter and a professor, she inspired several generations of aspiring artists who attended UCSC. Hardly a week went by without a former student contacting her to thank her for what she taught them. Additionally, she was a founding member of the Penny University, a weekly discussion group held in downtown Santa Cruz for over thirty years. She passed away in January, 2002.

The dirt road squeezes between towering redwood trees, decorated with tricycles, children's rocking horses and odd pieces of art resting on tree stumps. Twisting back and forth in a series of ever sharper and steeper curves, the road continues upward until it suddenly bursts out onto green fields. Horses gallop wildly alongside my car, their hoofs sending clumps of grass flying.

Well-ordered rows of grapes stretch across the ridge top, and at the crest of a knoll, tumbledown buildings rise with a two-story tower in the center, recalling an observation post in some mythical, long lost fortress. Climbing the rickety stairs to a house next to a barn, I find an open door. Inside the silent house, I find paintings and modern sculptures consisting of human figures. A partly-completed, larger-than-life horse's head leans against the wall and utilitarian furniture basks in the sunshine streaming in the window. No one appears to be home.

Outside, a gate opens onto an untended herb garden, next

door to another two-story house of recycled wood, its gabled roofs and ornate windows engineered by a fairy from a distant land. Lost, I climb back into my car and proceed to the top of the hill, passing rusted-out cars, bicycles and old stoves surrounded by waist-high grass. The bright pink blossoming cherry trees turn the air fragrant. A trail leads around the house and there, in the living room before a rock fireplace, I find Mary Holmes, smiling and radiant in the warmth of a blazing fire. Two dogs rush to greet me, their tails wagging.

A legend in Santa Cruz, Mary is one of the founding faculty members of UCSC, having come with Page Smith in 1965. Mary taught art history and theory to thousands of students in her 20 years of teaching at UCSC, before she retired at age 75. She says this morning she received several letters from students thanking her for teaching them; one she taught 30 years ago at the University of Ohio is now a professor, and another, from UCSC, is studying for a Ph. D. at Stanford.

Her white hair is neatly combed and two cats rest at her feet. Although in a wheelchair, she offers me tea and shares the story of what she considers her remarkably lucky life. She refers to a nearby painting, which illustrates her debt to Lady Luck. The central panel of a triptych shows Fortuna, the goddess of fortune, throwing dice. Fortuna is watched in the opposing panels by a man and woman looking into each other's eyes, opposite a woman, who stands alone. A quotation from Blake states, "Some are born to sweet delight, some are born to end with night, and it's a matter of fortune."

Born in Aberdeen, South Dakota in 1910, Mary grew up with her older sister and college-educated parents. Her mother's family came from a small community on the eastern shore of Maryland, a community unchanged from the 18th century, now largely disappeared. Her Irish/English grandfather on her mother's side of the family was a doctor who owned slaves. Her father's side of the family, which included many "preachers, teachers and heretics," dates back to 1626. Mary's father's father was an ardent abolitionist who maintained a station on the underground railroad. Obadia Holmes, another of her father's relatives, became famous for preaching adult baptism and being publicly horsewhipped in Boston because he refused to pay a fine for preaching his beliefs.

"His whipping gave the subsequent Holmes's a belief in being disagreeable," laughs Mary. "It's part of our tradition to express opinions that others don't agree with or express. My sister and I grew up with the sense that Holmeses had an obligation to hold beliefs, to announce them to the world, and not to compromise."

Her ancestors took opposing views on the role of Great Britain in the American colonies, as wells as on the issue of slavery. Her mother's family sided with the British during the Revolutionary War, while other members of the Holmes family were marooned on a ship and set to sea without food and water. These opposing viewpoints came up often when her parents fought the Civil War and the Revolutionary War "over and over again."

"I always advise people to marry someone they disagree with because it keeps life interesting," Mary says. "It certainly worked for my parents and they lived to be quite old. My father was 98 and my mother 96 when they died. Their minds were still sharp and they argued all the time."

Her mother and father were both schoolteachers, but with the explosion of opportunity in the early 1900s, her father took a job with the Chicago and Milwaukee railroad. He bought up right-of-ways and tried to convince people to buy land in South Dakota, which he predicted would be transformed from a dusty, desolate plain into a Garden of

Eden with the coming of the railroad.

At age four, Mary's family moved to a Chicago suburb on Lake Shore Drive, little more than a village at the time, where she attended a Montessori school. She jokes that the Montessori school ruined her life because she learned that she didn't have to learn anything she didn't want to learn. Although she was to spend the rest of her life in the academy, what she wanted to learn initially was quite limited; she only wanted to learn about horses and dogs. Although her interests broadened as she grew older, she remains fascinated by animals, especially horses and dogs.

"I love animals," she explains. "I think there's a gene for loving animals and you either have it or you don't. Animals are the greatest value for people; we learn from them. Animals will disappear in a couple hundred years, and it will be an unbelievable loss, for they are mythological creatures. I couldn't bear to live without a dog, with its wagging tail and wet nose. It's very real."

As a child, Mary indulged her love for animals when she returned to her grandmother's house on the eastern shore of Maryland each summer. She had dogs and cats, and her father bought her and her sister a pony from the famous wild herds on Chincoteague Island in Virginia.

"When I was six, my idea of riding a pony was to get on at the house and gallop to the barn. I was usually thrown off and the pony continued on to the barn. I led the pony back to the house and began again. At the end of the summer, the pony was still unbroken. I think it entertained the pony more than it did me."

Mary describes her childhood as being very narrow. Her mother stayed home while her father often went away on railroad business. In the fourth grade, she transferred from Montessori to public school. Little happened in school to impress her until her second year in high school, when she went away to Hanna Moore Academy, outside Baltimore. Her grandmother had attended this preparatory school named for an early feminist. She liked school but wasn't an outstanding student due to poor eyesight. Her problem wasn't discovered for some time because her doctor uncle wrote a letter saying she was in perfect health, although he had never examined her.

Despite the teacher's work on the blackboard being indecipherable to her, Mary did "well-enough" in school. When she attended college in Hollings, Virginia, she excelled in art because impressionism was in vogue and she couldn't paint details. She majored in philosophy, minored in French, and followed her own direction in painting, which her teachers loved.

"A bit of luck," claims Mary. "I was a perfect impressionist painter with no idea that my abilities were physiological. I turned my poor eyesight to my advantage. Everyone thought I was an artist, so I quietly slipped into the mold without any pain or agony."

After graduating from college, Mary's sister asked her to accompany her to Hamburg, Germany, where she had a college scholarship. Mary readily agreed and spent the next year attending concerts and museums. Through other Americans, she met a man in his thirties who discovered she was an artist. He confessed that he was ignorant about art and asked her to educate him. "What makes art great?" he asked. For three months she took him to the museums and explained art to him, but he abruptly told her they couldn't continue to see each other. She was saddened to discover later the man was a priest and she suspected that his superiors thought there was something improper about their relationship.

"It was pure comedy," laughs Mary. "I didn't know anything

at all about art except what I knew automatically. This poor man's art education was very spotty. It may not have been valuable for him but going around to the museums and clarifying what I considered the greatest works of art was valuable for me. Talking about art and art history became my life and it was great training. I had a degree in philosophy. Can you image anything more worthless?"

Germany was in the midst of the post-World War I depression and Mary returned home. Finding a job was nearly impossible, but that didn't bother her in the least. Young women of the time weren't expected to hold jobs and even if they wanted one, there were no jobs. She returned to Baltimore, where she met Max Brëdel, considered the greatest medical illustrator of the time for his work on Gray's Anatomy. Although he normally only took eight medical students, Mary's interest in esthetic issues intrigued him, and he allowed her to become one of his students. Like most scientists since Leonardo da Vinci, Brëdel insisted that his students learn anatomy first hand by dissecting a male and a female corpse. Mary found the process mysterious, profound, and more difficult than she imagined. Her first assignment was to draw a bone.

"We had a black and white piece of paper before us on an easel," she recalls. "A bone was suspended in front of a piece of black paper, and a piece of white paper, which we were to draw on, was placed next to it. We were to draw the bone exactly as we saw it, complete with the black background. I sat down and made a rapid sketch and thought I was through, but I was wrong. Every little hole in the bone had to be drawn. Six weeks later, working four hours a day, I finished. Most artists wouldn't have had the patience for this, but I was grateful to my teacher because he taught me to see."

When a friend of her sister's opened a restaurant in

the basement of a house in a residential neighborhood in Baltimore, Mary went to work for her. They never knew who would show up for dinner. Mary settled into working and drawing until a friend who wanted to study medicine asked her to go to Madison, Wisconsin and help her open a boarding house. Her parents lived nearby on a farm in Northern Iowa and Mary often visited them so she could ride horses and enjoy the outdoors. Meanwhile, Mary cooked for the eight boarders, while her friend continued medical school. The rest of the time she painted in her top floor studio. She recalls madcap adventures when she rushed downstairs to prepare meals at the last minute, leaving her paintings to dry upstairs.

At 26, Mary married and had a child, Michael, who was born in 1937. Although she dated some, she never took it seriously, because art absorbed all her attention. Additionally, her attendance at the women's college limited contact with men her own age. After college, it wasn't easy for an older woman to meet men in those days. Her marriage lasted two years.

"I didn't understand what my husband was like except on the surface, and he had no idea of who I was. I didn't understand who I was either, so how could anyone else? Unfortunately, the marriage didn't last but we have a marvelous son from the relationship."

Now a single mother, Mary focused on supporting herself. When she received an offer from a preparatory school to teach English, she took it, despite the $400 a year salary. The poor pay made her realize that she had to get an advanced degree to support herself and her son. An article in Life magazine described admissions to the University of Iowa master's degree program based on the submission of three paintings. She submitted the paintings and was accepted. When she arrived, she discovered that she also had to do course work.

The Midwest was experiencing an art revival at the time, based on the work of Grant Wood and Thomas Hart Benton, who proposed an American renaissance based on a style that became known as American Gothic. Grant Wood hoped to establish his home in Iowa City as the base of the revival. He was taken aback when a rival, Lester Longman, arrived from Princeton, the bastion of conventional art history, to take over Iowa's art department.

"Grant Wood had just made a great name for himself," Mary recalls. "He planned on turning the university into an apprentice program for himself. It was an extraordinary moment because he was famous and anything he said or did had immediate media value. Yet, everything he said was the opposite of what Iowa wanted. He was against all French painting, which is to say modern painting, and he was irreconcilable to the idea of compromising. There was a big battle between Grant Wood and Lester Longman."

Although Mary became friends with both men, she became a graduate student teaching assistant for Longman. Her apprenticeship in art history consisted of showing hundreds of slides — 300 a day, three days a week — to undergraduate classes. Slides flew by rapidly and she lectured students on the artists, and their paintings. She considered the process a wonderful learning method and prided herself on giving lectures to three sections of the class each week without repeating herself. Rather than taking the MFA program, which she considered flaky, she took the regular Master's Program, which included hands-on experience painting and sculpting.

"Lester Longman believed that every painter had to know art history and every art historian had to be able to paint," she says. "There was no use in accumulating evidence about art if you didn't know what painting and sculpting were like and could show some talent by presenting your own work. It was an extraordinary moment in the academic world."

After graduation, she continued to teach at Iowa and, when W.W. II began, and professors began to be drafted, she took over their classes, sometimes in the middle of the semester. Although she might know little about a course, she quickly had to step in to teach, which forced her to learn even more about the history of art.

After the war, Frank Seiberling asked her to come to Ohio to head the art department and she accepted. One of her most memorable experiences from this time — again what she calls the intervention of Lady Luck — was taking responsibility, along with two other professors, for a TV station in Columbus, Ohio. Before the penetration of ABC, CBS and NBC, small independent stations oversaw their own programs. No one knew what to program for the public, and without guidelines, Mary and the other professors improvised by giving lectures and adding musicians to the program. This was a challenge as they also had to provide content while learning the technology behind TV, and other skills necessary to production such as lighting and filming.

In 1954, Gibson Danes, the head of the art department at UCLA, asked her to come there and teach, but warned that they couldn't offer her a tenured position.

"I didn't care about tenure and didn't want to teach someplace that didn't want me," Mary asserts. "I was always happy to go someplace and offend people, so I accepted the job. I've always told the truth and sometimes people got offended. Sometimes a piece of canvas is only a piece of canvas and an artist shouldn't paint anything on it if he's not in the right relationship to it. Then it should stay in the closet. But no, they have to have some gimmick and paint on it and then hang it up for everyone to see. So much of contemporary art is a gimmick. I was talking to one artist who didn't have anything to say and then I saw that he'd glued clothing on the canvas and became famous for it. See, he found his gimmick. Art is in a terrible position today."

Mary taught art history and art theory at UCLA, concentrating on art works that the texts missed or left out. She provided the background to reveal the matrix out of which art arises. For her, art is concerned with reality, but reality is a shifting phenomenon. Sometimes the only things that are real are the things people can't see. In this case, the artist takes on the difficult task of enabling others to see. The artists then become highly valued for such skills because "seeing is believing." Artists constitute the basis of faith by revealing what's invisible, for example, the infinite value of the soul or the depths of hell, saints or angels. Talented artists are given a power to imagine what others can't imagine, but long to see. In this way, artists play an important role in society.

"The worst thing that ever happened to art is the idea of personal expression," Mary claims. "Art is always personal expression and never is. Every single thing we do bares the mark, or the act, of us doing it but, if you dislike someone, the more they appear to you the more you dislike them until every little thing they do infuriates you. Our uniqueness makes us despair of each other. I used to think that I'd know all the answers when I got to be an adult, but I found out that adults don't know either. Now I think that when I die, I'll know. I haven't tried that yet."

At UCLA, Mary met Page Smith at a faculty luncheon, when the administration was trying to break down departmental isolation. She found they both liked a famous three-volume set of art books, and Page gave her the volumes because he had an extra set. When he invited her to dinner, she discovered that his wife, Eloise Pickard, was the sophisticated classically beautiful woman she once had admired in a Santa Monica super market. The two women got along famously, and the three became good friends. When Dean McHenry invited Page Smith to UCSC in 1965, he said he wouldn't come unless Mary Holmes came too. A perplexed and baffled McHenry agreed.

"It was a wonderful, marvelous time," recalls Mary. "The sixties were a turning point. We all thought it was our fault that people came to class without shoes or shirts or serious intent. We thought we'd caused this, but it had nothing to do with us; it was the times. The students had a terrible time fulfilling their passions because there was no administration to fight; no one was oppressing them. They'd come in with a list of demands and Page would say fine, let's try it. If they wanted classes in poetry or power engines, we'd work out the lectures and offer the courses. It was a wonderful time to teach, but I always enjoyed teaching no matter what period. I tried to show students the best art and pass over the mediocre. People were so grateful to get help in viewing paintings. They got a deep joy from knowing about art."

Soon UCSC gained a reputation for being an innovative institution that attracted creative vigorous and passionate teachers from other colleges. Mary admits that some were "nut cases with varying degrees of charm" but feels that every institution needs a certain number of nuts to give it character.

Mary continued teaching and painting, although her subject remained women throughout her career. She doesn't know what it means, perhaps narcissism, and she doesn't care. Although she feared that her art would be seen as too eccentric, it was enough for her to have her work recognized in a number of California art shows as being on a professional level.

Mary retired at age 75 in 1985 and settled on her

mountaintop outside Soquel where she enjoyed the forest, the open fields, her animals and riding her horses. She stopped riding horses, but she continued to enjoy open fires, the sunshine streaming in her windows and her dogs and cats. She was clear and bright, a joy to be with, especially when she laughed and talked about Lady Luck, who was her guardian angel.

The end
Copyright
Monkerud, 2018

Chapter 4: Jami Cassady
The Barn Gave Me a Gift

Everybody knew The Barn — you could see it from the freeway, and there it was, spelled out in big letters, The Barn. I loved it. I would dress up in a paisley, V-neck shirt with belled sleeves - the one I shared with Chris Gies and my younger brother, John. It was the only item of hippy clothing we owned.

This was '67, and my boyfriend Peter's band was the house band there. I cannot believe Peter and I went to the 8 am every weekend ... I was 17.

I met Peter through my younger brother. John was in a ton of bands in the mid-60s; the first of which was with his good friends Mike Dyer, Dave Goddard, Mark Slemmons, and Peter Curry. Peter was the drummer. We were all from the Los Gatos-Saratoga area, but their band played a lot in Santa Cruz. I was a year older than John and his friends, Peter was closer to my age. When I stopped dating Mike, Peter and I got together.

Peter then became the drummer for Bubble with Ken Craft and Alan Smith and Bubble became the house band at The Barn. Peter would come over to the house in Los Gatos every Friday and Saturday night in his VW bus with all the instruments in the back. I remember sitting in the living room by the fire at my mother's house on Bancroft Avenue, waiting and watching out the front window for the bus to appear.

We had to drive over Highway 17 in the VW bus with all that stuff in the back to get to The Barn. I cannot believe my mom allowed me to do that, but we did it. We'd cruise in that bus from Los Gatos to Scotts Valley, and that was a crazy thing to do. I mean, you can die a horrible death on that highway. Highway 17 ... We were young and smoking pot and drinking, and then for twenty-five minutes we navigated through the twists and turns of the Santa Cruz Mountains. No seat belts back then, but, hey, "Let's go."

Everybodyy went to The Barn. It was a magical place with that Avalon or Fillmore vibe. There was a big bar on the main floor, and up top was a huge dance floor where the band played while the lights zoomed. When we went to The Barn, I'd be gone all night. It was an all-night happening, especially for the house band. Peter would go upstairs and do his band thing from the moment we arrived. I'd wander around, or sit at the bar. I remember hoisting my butt upon the barstools, but I can't remember what l drank — I know that I hated beer back then.

I also know that The Barn was always a warm, welcoming place. There were antiques all over — I think they were leftovers from when it was a flower shop. There was something to notice on every wall and in every corner. There was so much room in there ... You could sit in a chair and read, and I'm sure people were taking LSD, but I did not know about that then. To me, it was just very comforting to be there. I felt part of the whole at The Barn. Maybe it was because I was the house drummer's girl. Maybe it was because I was there every weekend among fellow free spirits. Maybe it was because I was on my own, away from the eagle-eye of my mom. And, maybe it was because I knew the owner.

Leon Tabory and I were tight. I didn't know much about his personal life at that time — I didn't know he was a Holocaust survivor, I didn't know he had kids or was married, but he'd been a part of my life since I was ten years old. Leon was family to me because of his connection to my dad, Neal Cassady.

When my dad was serving time in San Quentin, Leon was his psychologist. They became really good friends, and Leon wanted to continue to help dad after parole. He did, and he got fired for it, so he lived with us for a while at the Los Gatos house. Mom always welcomed in the guys connected to Neal, and there was always a party on Bancroft Avenue. It was just my reality to have people coming in and out of the house. Whether it was Leon, Big Daddy Nord, Ferlinghetti, or Kesey. there was no invitation required. The guys just showed up, and mom tried to make everyone happy with pizza and a gallon of wine.

I'm pretty sure Mom never went to The Barn, though. By 1967, she was really involved in the community, creating her own life after she and dad divorced. Dad was on his own, but after the divorce, he'd still come to the Los Gatos house to rejuvenate ... he'd sleep, and mom would fix him soup. I remember she'd tell him, "Get down off that mountain in La Honda and get some rest," and he would.

I can't recall if I had seen dad at The Barn any time before that one time at the end of 1967. I guess it's possible, since the Further bus was often parked outside, but I really only have one distinct memory. I met dad on the main floor. He stumbled in, and I noticed him right away. "Let's go downstairs, away from the scene," I said. I could tell be had that look, like he needed help, so I said, "Come, dad, let's go." He crawled into one of those catacomb-like spaces with the pillows and the blankets. I followed. I had never gone into one of those before at The Barn, but that night I followed dad to that place where we shut out the world, and it was just the two of us lying there together.

He was gaunt with a stubbled chin, and I knew he was out of it and hallucinating. But he was also lucid, and it felt so healing because despite it all, I knew he knew who I was. He was moving his head back and forth, up and down, and as he looked all around with those acid eyes, he saw me —

he recognized me. Eventually, he settled down, and we just hugged and hugged. I felt so much love. Then, he fell asleep, so I carried that tender moment with me as I walked up the stairs to hear the band and take in the light show.

I never saw my dad again. About a month later, his life would end near the train tracks just outside San Miguel de Allende, Mexico.

I didn't realize it at the time. but I know now that our souls were saying goodbye that night. So, while I am certain that The Barn was a gift to lots of flower children of that era, The Barn gave me a gift for which I'll forever be grateful. That's where I got to say goodbye to my dad.

Chapter 5: Rick Alan
Cathy Puccinelli Interview

We're sitting here with an old, dear friend, Cathy Puccinelli, whom I've known since we were kids in the '60s. We wanted to hear about some of her memories of those years, so Cathy, welcome to the Hip History Project.

Cathy: Thanks Rick. Rick and I have known each other for 50 years.

HH: It's a big number.

C: Yes! (Laughs) I wanted to begin by saying I am a native. My father had a business in town. He sold Jeeps. Earlier, he sold Frasers, Simcas, Alpha Romeos, but on a very small scale of course, and he had a shop with mechanics. So, I was raised here. Both my grandmothers were a big influence, I think, on who I am today. My grandmother Rosa made the ravioli for the Santa Cruz Hotel. I have fond memories of pinching the stuffing into ravioli and pinching them closed. My other grandmother Hattie was a seamstress. She made the costumes for the Seniorama! Can you believe that it's still going on? And I'd like to just mention on how different the environment was when I was growing up here in Santa Cruz. We had lots and lots of really big trees. I remember, as a little girl, walking along the river, which was not yet confined in the Army Corp levees, with the high banks. It was a river — a swift river sometimes and a gentle river at other times, and it had sandy beaches. I would walk with my grandmother in the sand and pick up the big Sycamore leaves. I have fond memories of that — probably through old photos and videos. Um, so the town was very different. There were many vacant lots, and very little traffic, maybe a little bit in the summer.

I remember the '55 flood, and my father holding me on his shoulders, watching as the river gobbled his cars and took them to the sea, and my father saying "did you see that, Poochie, did you see that?"

Really cool, you know. It was a tragedy, but my father never took difficulties that hard, he always came back.

HH: He was resilient.

C: He was resilient, yes. I think being from an immigrant's family, being an immigrant's son, he learned that resiliency. So, I graduated from high school…

HH: Which one?

C: Santa Cruz High School, 1967, and fell in love with a man — before I graduated — who was making sandwiches at the Catalyst and, uh, he was a very young man too, and we got married the year after I graduated. I will say this: you know, there was a lot of pot around during my high school years…

HH: Excuse me, your high school years covered from '63 to '67

C: Yes…

HH: That's right through the transition period:

C: Yes! As a matter of fact, our neighbors often had the Merry Prankster's bus parked in their driveway…

HH: Where were you living at that point?

C: On a little one-lane road in what became Carbonero. My father built a house there. We built our house in '55 and the neighbors built theirs, I think, five years later.

HH: The Prankster's knew somebody who lived next door?

C: Well, our neighbors had six children, and the oldest, Laurie, fell in love with one of the Pranksters. We were going up to the City to hear Janis and we were very involved with the music scene in San Francisco — our parents didn't know this of course — but getting back to what we were talking about…

HH: You were talking about high school…

C: Oh, well, I wanted to mention that we were talking earlier about how this was a very conservative city, very

Republican town, and actually I don't think so. I would say that there were equal numbers of Republicans and Democrats, with a few outliers — there were John Birchers and on the other side there were the real lefties. These were people who could speak to one another, who could talk to one another, who could be on a city council together and come together on things and although my parents were very conservative I feel that, although I left most of that behind, I took away some very good things.

I started my married life as a hippie girl, really — I didn't have much education. Then I took some classes at Cabrillo. I took some of the first feminist classes; I subscribed to *Ms. Magazine* and *High Times,* (laughs) and *Rolling Stone.* So, rents were cheap. We struggled to pay eighty dollars a month, but we lived down by the river and we were happy. Even thought this movement was in between the beatnik movement — I guess you would say and — and whatever it evolved into — I never felt that people were unkind. We were the beautiful people—we were young and beautiful.

HH: During your high school years what do you remember about some of the places around town, like the Catalyst, Hip Pocket, the Barn, etc.

C: I guess I still have a decent memory. I was in my junior or senior year in high school and I was actually hired — I don't remember if it was Peter Demma — it must have been, and I got hired to do some inventory. He put me in the art section, which was right next to the erotic section — I remember that vividly. (Laughs) And, of course, I met Mark Skomsvold, who would later become my husband — he was a sandwich maker there…

HH: At the Catalyst?

C: At the Catalyst. You could walk right through a mirrored room. There was a fountain in the room. As a matter of fact

John Tuck married us in that room. There were a few other people — Al DiLudovico and Patty and I think Al van Zyl and Tom Scribner were there. Anyway, the bookstore was hooked together with the Catalyst and later when bands started playing there I was still too young to go into the bar.

HH: Did you and Mark or friends ever go up to the Barn in Scotts Valley?

C: Yes, we went up there several times I'd say. One time in particular, I remember there was a lot of acid being taken, so we did that and a moonlight walk. There was mescaline and lots of lights, strobe lights. Uh, at that time there was a lot of pot, people smoking pot, and also cocaine. Coke had really started to come into town. And also diet pills. Women were using diet pills. Really edgy drugs were coming in, compared to pot. The pot hadn't developed into what it is today. However there were some pot growers that I came across that I learned some things from. You could grow some really good buds in Santa Cruz, though it was illegal, *really illegal*. They could confiscate your property at that time — there was always that fear.

So, things changed for me a little bit — not a little bit, a lot, when I gave birth, and I was not involved with much hallucinogenic drugs or speed or anything like that. It was my choice not to get involved in those things, but I did like pot. I liked gardening, so wherever I went I would plant. A little side story: for a time I lived on Otis St., 111 Otis St.

HH: that was just down the block from Ralph Abraham who lived on California St.

C: Yeah, he had a great big Victorian. I didn't know him. I only knew him as someone from the university who had bought property. So I lived on Otis St. and that was the first house that I bought because my grandfather had died and left me nine thousand dollars. So I paid three thousand dollars and the city made me tear down the little historic wooden building along side it because they thought it was a rattrap, and that's where I put my garden. The story is that someone had given me all these poppy seeds, beautiful poppy seeds, and I grew beautiful poppies, and *Sunset Magazine* did an article on gardens in Santa Cruz and I was included and had a picture of the flowers in the article, and it turned out they were opium poppies — so I got a visit and had to take out all the poppies. (Laughs) I think that was about the time I met you — you were coming over to the house. I met Rick when he… did you live at Blaine St.?

HH: Yep. Myself, Steve and Pat Dinkelakker and Chuck Garner found the place. And John Munoz moved in. That's where we started the Free Spaghetti Dinner.

C: Chucko! Souixe Campbell wasn't there then?

HH: No, Souixe didn't come to Blaine St. until about a year later. We settled in there about '68.

C: Anyway, I had a beautiful garden. I had a geodesic dome my dad helped put up in the back and I grew there. And when I had the opportunity I moved to my grandparents' place. My father's parents had bought a property off of Golf Club Dr. near the Tannery. My father had tried to sell it several times but no one wanted it. To live near the Tannery — it was very smelly. All those hides, it was…

HH: Heavy chemical action?

C: Heavy chemicals. My grandfather worked for the Tannery and he worked in logging. My grandmother worked in the canneries when they got here from Italy. My grandparents, Giuseppe and Rosa met on the boat coming over from Genoa. My grandmother was supposed to drop off with her brothers in Bogota but they fell in love, and, accompanied by her two brothers and my grandfathers' brother and sister, they landed in San Francisco where they married. The Puccinellis moved here and were land tenant farmers and then eventually purchased the farm. We always called it the farm but my dad called it the ranch; but it was being farmed so it became "The Farm", and I lived there for forty years, until recently.

HH: For our Hip History readers, if you drive up Golf Club Dr., just before you go up the hill to the Pogonip trail head, if you look to the left you'll see a grand, old two-story, red farmhouse, and a big pasture where crops were, and are raised, and I believe where your father was born…

C: No, he was born at the fire station out on Seventh Avenue. They were tenant farmers but eventually became tenants and then bought the land. It hadn't been farmed for many years. Cows were raised in the pasture.

My father had polio when he was four and his father died when my dad was young. My Nonna would take him to Cowells Beach and have him soak his legs in the ocean while she worked in the Cannery. She would check on him during her breaks as he was left alone. He became a good swimmer although his leg had no muscle, and he wore a special shoe with a five inch heel. When I was young he would take me swimming at New Brighton. I'd be on his back and we'd go really far out.

Dad was friends with Steinbeck! And Doc Ricketts also. And a famous artist who painted scenes of the coast. L. E. DeJoiner. Dad traded him a truck for one of his paintings!

When I moved to the ranch I began to farm it and my first farming episode was a disaster. I planted pumpkins and corn. The deer ate the corn and the pumpkins — I didn't turn over — I was not a farmer. But Dennis Tamura approached me from the University. I think he had graduated from the Chadwick program, and he asked me if I thought this would be a great place for leafy green vegetables and if he could farm it and I said yes. He began farming and then moved off several years later. He now has the Blue Heron Farms in Watsonville, a large organic farm operation, one of the first. And my farm became sort of an incubating farm for young farmers. Over the years I probably had six different farms on the property. The last was the *Dirty Girls* farm that became pretty famous for their dry-farmed tomatoes. Jim Denevan farmed here and decided he was not going to shovel manure, that wasn't his thing, and he began *Outstanding in the Field* while he was out standing in my field. He decided he was going to put on dinners. I think my farm hosted six farm dinners through that involvement.

HH: So you moved on to the ranch — was that before or after Annie Steinhart and those folks moved out there?

C: Oh, yes! My dad had rented the farm — and they called it "Rancho…"

HH: Retardo? Back before it was politically incorrect?

C: Retardo! Annie Steinhart, Duke — with the snake — and the fellow who started the Mountain Store in Boulder Creek…

HH: And John Bogle, the potter?

C: Yes, John… and Bruce Anderson lived next door to me — I loved Bruce Anderson. He was a very well known potter and he and I became very close friends.

When I first moved there a steer had been left in the field and I insisted I didn't want any slaughtering done, so I had this Holstein living in the field — he lived about sixteen years — we named him Peterbuilt. He was breaking out all the time. He would go around in the morning and scratch his head on every fence post and the posts would all give way at the same time. He would escape often and I would go to take my daughter Heather to school and we would have to go round him up first. We once found him down on River St.

Peterbuilt loved classical music and when Bruce would

play classical music in the morning, with his cup of coffee, Peterbuilt would break out and go searching for Bruce. One day Bruce called me and said "Cathy, you have to come now, there's a bull in my china cabinet." (Laughs)

HH: So, you moved there after Annie and that group had moved out?

C: Yes, I moved there in 1975, on one of the hottest days of the year — it was 104 degrees — and I moved out a few years ago, on one of the hottest days of the year. Full circle. But that was forty years.

HH: I want to return to the '60s for a moment. Many of the kids I lived with at Avalon St., 7th Ave. House, etc. were very central, in my memory, to the Santa Cruz Hip scene. These were kids who went to Santa Cruz High, or SLV High, some to Soquel High, when it opened in '62. Can you talk a little about what was going on the campuses for teens as the culture was rapidly transforming?

C: We had some fabulous teachers that came to Santa Cruz when the university came to town. Jim Goodhue was our literature teacher. Mary Duffield, who had been in Santa Cruz for quite awhile. Teachers influenced their student's lives. Mary was one who affected me, Jim Goodhue, as well; Mr. Davenport; and they were all very progressive, poetic people in my mind, made a big impact, especially when you come from an environment that was working class, where you had to really put your nose to the grindstone to make something of your life, which is true of anything I suppose, but you don't have to "grind it up"; once you find what you love, whatever that is, you can figure out how to make it not such a grind.

HH: And so you were literally growing up right here in Santa Cruz when things were changing so fast…

C: Oh, I'm still growing up! (Laughs)

HH: (Laughs) Yes, but we were still kids, things were in an

actual transformation…the university opened in late '65…

C: Well I was still living with my family then. It was the time of the Beatles, the Rolling Stones. My father took me up to the Beatles concert. He was good about that. I was smoking pot then but I don't think he knew it, but we needed a driver. It took a lot longer to get to the City in those days — well, it might actually take longer now to get into the City.

HH: Did you go to the Beatles concert in Candlestick Park?

C: Yes! I saw the Stones. Janis Joplin. I went to the Fillmore, the Avalon Ballroom. But I loved going to school. I joined SNCC. (Laughs) I really didn't know what I was doing. I got to work on the (student) Trident Newspaper. I loved writing poetry. Those were all things that were outside of the box of how my family was.

HH: How was your family handling all this?

C: My family was experiencing difficulties with mental illness. My brother was diagnosed as a paranoid schizophrenic. And he was having problems since he was about twelve. There were a lot of people and drugs coming into Santa Cruz. But I think he first started sniffing glue. Remember you used to be able to put airplanes together with glue. You can't do that now. He also started smoking pot. Then I think he stopped doing any drugs. He was definitely showing signs of mental illness and hallucinations and it was really difficult for my family. It's a difficult time for any family with mental illness. There's a history of mental illness in my family and I think my father thought it was hopeless but my mother didn't. There were times I didn't want to go home because my father's car would be parked there and that meant my brother probably had been acting out. But my family never abandoned my brother. He's dead now but he lived as a chronic schizophrenic all his life and he took medication. At that time Stelazine and Thorazine were pretty much it.

Lithium seemed to help him in the later years. He was sent to different "asylums", as they were called. And there I was, getting married, involved in the hippie scene, the psychedelic scene — my parents — I'm amazed we stayed so close. We never lost touch. My dad loved me and he loved hanging around the farm. My mother taught me the love of antiques.

I think the essence of life really is love. I see in Santa Cruz how many people have been abandoned, people that have mental illness, abandoned not just by their family — because I can see how easy it could be to abandon someone who is mentally ill. They're sometimes scary, sometimes very dangerous and you don't have the knowledge, the support systems. I can see how that happens. However, all these people we see that are mentally ill that we see walking on our streets — they have a family, a parent a grand parent — maybe not. Maybe they were foster children, wards of the court, I don't know, but we, as a society, we have abandoned them. We in Santa Cruz, we have a burden placed on us because we've tried to help, and I think it's unfortunate we haven't put enough resources into it, especially in the very beginning, when homelessness was increasing.

I walked the railroad tracks where I lived many times and I would clean up and talk to the women along the track and hear how they had just got out of jail and the first thing they want to do is get high. I'd talk to them about treatment programs. Many of them had ten, twelve programs they'd been through. I don't know what the answer is but I know we still have to respect the mentally ill, to take care of them.

HH: At the end of the '60s the press was calling us the "murder capital of the world". The Haight got mean and ugly in '67 and '68. How did that affect you? Did you see that as an aspect of the cultural shift that had so rapidly transformed things? I always thought of it as part of the mix.

C: I didn't. I remember the Ohta family murders, Herb Mullin. Kemper. But I didn't think of that as part of the mix. I do remember a drug dealer in Bonny Doon who murdered his wife.

HH: What about some of the cultural scene, nightlife, music in Santa Cruz in those years?

C: I remember backpacking in the Big Sur Mountains, going to Esalen. Seeing Joan Baez, Mimi Farina, Bob Dylan. I remember locally, the Catalyst was always good for music. I remember the Grass Cookie, which is now Moe's Alley.

Baba Ram Dass — I can't say I was a follower — I just took in what he said. The book "Be Here Now", I bought it and still have it. I will never give it away. Maybe to my grandkids. I remember seeing him when he came to Santa Cruz. I was literally projected out of this world, to somewhere, I don't know where, and then I came back with this incredible feeling of being… uh, lifted, I don't know…

HH: Elevated?

C: Elevated, yeah. It felt good. I won't say enlightened because I don't feel I'm enlightened, but I'm so appreciative of people who can pull things out of you, you know? And that's what he does for me; he pulls things out of me that I like.

HH: You told me you saw him in the City when you were younger.

C: Yes, in a very small space. I don't remember the name of the hall. The Merry Pranksters were up there. And one of them, a sandal maker named Bob and Laurie and I went to see him. He had either just come back from or was just going to India, to either stop talking or begin talking. I forget. (Laughs) One of those sojourns. I think it was before he went and stopped talking. And later, when he started talking again, I remember hearing him speak and he said "you know, when you don't talk it's really easy to get women". He was trying to be funny. In the same talk, he said he'd had to go back to New York because his father and mother had died and he was closing down their apartment. His father died before his mother and had kept all of his father's shoes high up in the closet, in boxes. And as he was taking them down he would open the boxes and look at his father's shoes, and all these memories came back with all these sets of shoes. There he was. Who he really was as a person, sitting there, the son of this man with all of these shoes. I just loved the way he would put things together that way.

H: Do you remember the Sticky Wicket?

C: I do! We went there to hear jazz, down in Aptos I think. I wasn't of age but my neighbors went there. I think, due to my personality, I wasn't too involved out there. I wasn't too outgoing, not too involved in a lot of events locally. Although, later my career took off because I can be outgoing, so maybe, like many people, uh, I energize quietly at home.

HH: Then take it on the road?

C: Uh huh, because I am an initiator. That's why the farm survived. It was a beautiful piece of property. The folks that have it now, the Costanoan Commons, are really good people with good goals and I'm hoping the city will work with them.

HH: Cathy, you've been involved over the years with environmental actions and I wonder if you would talk about that.

C: Well, I lived just below Pogonip. Pogonip was purchased by the state for the city to have as a park and there was a developmental plan that was drawn up and I was part of that planning. There were various people from different parts of the community, with differing attitudes and ideas. We had to all come together on this project. We had many meetings at Harvey West and the public would come and comment and bring their input.

HH: This wasn't the original Green Belt Plan?

C: Yes. We drew up a Master Plan for Pogonip. I was part of that effort. I was involved with some other things. I was a volunteer with Parks and Rec. I led what I called "weed and water walks". Water is such an important resource that we have to keep healthy. And my own pet peeve — trash. I think we have one of the dirtiest cities I've come across, and I've traveled extensively in the United States and places far poorer than ours. For some reason we have so much trash. People don't seem to pick up the trash that's right out their front doors. I've walked the river with my dog, picking up trash but now I just do it closer to home.

I wanted to mention someone who's had a big impact on me over the years, certainly when I was leading tours in Pogonip: Brysis Buchanan. I think I did my first weed walk with her and she taught me the "seven universal weeds". She must have been in her eighties then. Anyway, she would take us for weed walks and it was always enjoyable and I'd have my little girl tagging along. I just wanted to mention her because there is a wildness that's out there in nature that this generation — the "device generation" I want to call it — is not involved with. My grandson is a device child. When they do get involved though they do get engaged. It is so cool! When they see Old Faithful going off or a cougar in the wild it has such a big impact. So any time you can get your device controlled kids away from their devices — do it! (Laughs)

HH: How do you remember the Vietnam War?

C: Oh. I…I, uh… I lost several — I won't say buddies, but boys I knew, classmates. I was so opposed. I remember writing poetry in the Trident — bring the boys home! I protested up in San Francisco and Berkeley, and I remember having my infant in my arms, standing next to a guy with a military style rifle, you know, keeping the crowds in line. I wasn't very active politically, but that was…you know, we're still fighting in Afghanistan — we're still fighting — and our current political climate is very sad and disappointing.

HH: We thought we were going to change the world. The war cast a pall over things — it was very difficult, very difficult… it's interesting to be talking here about the '60s and the promise it seemed to have held, for a hot minute…

C: We had the civil rights movement, the beginning of the feminist movement. But the government started attacking students on campuses. Hopefully that won't happen again, but it feels like anything could happen…

HH: Well, I think one of the virtues of the Hip History project is that gathering up people's memories and thoughts about those days when the world was changing fast can help us through dark times. It's so important to connect the past, present and future. Cathy, I want to thank you so much. It's wonderful to have your voice here.

C: Thank you.

Chapter 6: Don Monkerud
Scott Kennedy — A Lifetime Devoted to Nonviolence:

The following interview was conducted with Scott Kennedy at his dining room table in 2001 for a book of interviews, Santa Cruz, A Creative Community. *Scott was deeply involved in Santa Cruz politics, served on the City Council, and was an advocate of the rights of Palestinians. In addition, he played a key role at the Resource Center for Nonviolence, and took groups to the Middle East to promote peace and dialogue between Israelis and Palestinians. He brought a fresh, creative perspective to life and lived his ideals.*

Known for political activism, Santa Cruz was one of the first communities in the U.S. to ban nuclear weapons, a move aimed squarely at Lockheed Corporation, one of America's penultimate weapons manufacturers. The ban became a model for a national Nuclear Weapons Freeze, just as Santa Cruz protests against U.S. intervention in Central America became a model for a national Witness for Peace movement.

The Resource Center for Nonviolence helped kick off both of these efforts, and along with others, Scott Kennedy was there from the beginning.

In 1949 when one-year-old Scott Kennedy moved to San Jose's Willow Glen area, plum, cherry, and apricot orchards marched to the city's boundaries and bucolic rural scenes shouldered the small city's outlying areas. It was a time of peace and prosperity that left its mark on young Scott and played a role in his fervent devotion to nonviolence.

Of Scotch, Irish, English and German ancestry, Scott's parents left their families in Newman Grove, Nebraska, a farming town of 1000 northwest of Omaha, to seek a better life. His parents' fathers had both been mayor of the town and, during the depression, both experienced reversals in economic status. His mother's family lost their business, while his father's father acquired a Firestone tire dealership and Mobil oil distributorship. His father and mother were in the same class in school and attended the Methodist Church in a town that boasted seven protestant churches. Five children followed through the years, Scott being the youngest.

Scott's father took over the oil business from his father, but in 1948 his storage tanks burned and the city council, fearing another fire, would not allow him to install new ones, even underground.

Additionally, efforts to build a gymnasium for the local school ran into a tight-fisted, anti-tax school board that Scott's father felt relegated education and his children's futures to a minor role in the community. Meanwhile, his father's brother wrote enthusiastically from the Alameda Navy base about the excellent education system in California, wonderful mild weather and economic opportunity just waiting to be realized. The family packed up and headed west.

With money they received from selling their house in Nebraska, they purchased a four-bedroom home in the white middle-class suburb of Willow Glen for $25,000. Scott's father got a job as the sales manager at the Tire Service Company in San Jose, and he quickly became the top salesman. His mother became a housewife while Scott attended kindergarten, walked to school, and attended Willow Glen Elementary, Edwin Markham Junior High, and Willow Glen High School. He played team sports, had lots of friends, and lived what he considered a normal childhood.

"San Jose was a great place to grow up," said Scott. "By the time I got to school, my parents were on automatic pilot for parenting. Both extremes were already established in school — the oldest children in the family were achievers and the one next to me a troublemaker — so they were ready for whatever path I chose. I had a pretty banal middle-class upbringing; my dad was a workaholic and Mother was the mainstay of the family. My brother was experimentally pushing all the boundaries and I saw my parents struggling with him, so I didn't give them any trouble."

Although Scott's parents were not demonstratively religious and didn't emphasize a belief system, his father firmly believed that businesses should be honest and have integrity. His family's attendance at the local Methodist church and their values affected him. For example, he recalled a controversy his father had at work because his boss continually referred to black people as "N…." His father's protest fell on deaf ears until he began using anti-Italian slurs. The boss got the point and stopped using derogatory slurs.

When a family with a Peruvian mother and Scottish father attempted to buy a house on his block, the neighbors tried to prevent the sale. Scott's parents were outspoken in support of the family moving into the neighborhood and once they did, their son became Scott's closest friend. His parents also supported Scott's education, which included Friday afternoon religious instruction at the Methodist Church, and a school-sponsored citizenship training that included a savings account offered by Bank of America.

Scott's oldest sister, Diane, attended Stanford and shocked her family when she announced she was becoming a Methodist missionary and going to spend three years in Uruguay. "Good middle class kids just didn't go to weird foreign countries," Scott recalled. He corresponded with his sister in Uruguay by reel-to-reel tape, listening to and recording messages. She represented the only unusual person in his early years.

His school years were mundane, although he enjoyed social

studies, speech, debating classes, and French. It wasn't until high school that life became exciting.

"It was the beginning of the 60s and change was percolating through the schools," Scott said. "I came from a well-established family; I slept in the same bedroom from 1949 to 1966. I had lived a very different life than my friends and peers who had moved around a lot and whose parents broke up. It was the early part of the counter-cultural experience, and going to concerts and anti-war demonstrations was exciting. We traveled everywhere to hear musicians like The Doors and Joan Baez."

Scott and a group of disaffected friends, who called themselves "Cynics," thought they had an inside track on what was happening. They listened to bluegrass music and read books like *The Diary of Anne Frank* and Viktor Frankl's *Man's Search for Meaning*. Frankl's assertion that Nazi death camp survivors created something to live for — whether it was the next spring or their children — left a lasting impression on him.

He wanted to delve beneath the surface of the life he'd grown up with and realized meaning was more central to human experience than power or personal gratification.

Putting his beliefs to work, he helped publish *The Escalator*, an underground high school paper with the motto, "Escalate your mind, not the war." The editors were called into the principal's office and warned against distributing it at school. A friend with shoulder-length hair got picked on and called "faggot" by the high school football players and, when Scott defended him, they threatened to beat him up. By his junior year, he began dating his future wife, Kristin Champion, who lived three blocks away, and he had known since elementary school.

While attending the Methodist Church, Scott joined a

youth leadership program and became a representative to the San Jose District Youth Leadership Team. He cut class his senior year to hear Martin Luther King speak at Sproul Plaza, UC Berkeley, and attended services by Cecil Williams, in addition to attending anti-war and civil rights rallies, marches and talks. He wore a CORE (Congress of Racial Equality) button to class. In his senior year, he was elected student body president and immediately appointed previously unrepresented blacks, hippies and Latinos to student body commissions.

He saw that there was more to life than having a good time and, throughout high school, Scott worked and saved his money. Memorable jobs included working with his brother who drove a flower delivery truck. By his senior year, Scott worked two jobs, one at his father's tire store after school and in the summer, and at a Thrifty Drug Store at night. He claimed he "saved every nickel."

His religious involvement led him to consider a "calling to the ministry." After attending talks at church summer camp by conscientious objectors from W.W. II, Korea and Vietnam, he realized that Christianity rejects violence as a way to resolve conflicts. When he registered for the draft, he applied as a conscientious objector (C.O.).

"Applying for C.O. status was a watershed event in my life," said Scott. "It's difficult to step off the escalator of what's considered normal. The draft board turned down my application and I appealed. I have a vivid memory of going before my draft board and defending my case. They tried to talk me out of it.

"'You can go to the university or into the ministry and get a deferment,' the draft board said. 'Why go to all this trouble?' They suggested that I wait four years before making up my mind, and I told them that if they didn't give me the C.O.

classification, I'd drop out of school and go to jail before going into the military. I wanted them to rule immediately. They gave me the deferment. It definitely set my life in a certain direction."

Scott graduated from high school in 1967 and, while many of his friends enrolled at San Jose State and UC Berkeley, he applied to Stanford and UCSC. Accepted at UCSC, Scott began as a philosophy major in 1967. He lived on campus and immediately continued his involvement in anti-war activities, including the National Mobilization in San Francisco. Although he didn't use drugs, he attended the Rolling Stones Concert "Woodstock West" at Altamont. He and his future wife, Kris, who also attended UCSC, demonstrated in support of People's

Park in Berkeley, and joined a UCSC delegation to Sacramento to meet with Governor Ronald Reagan about the park.

"We were in a room with Ronald Reagan and I had the definite impression that he was mad," explained Scott. "He was disconnected and talked about the *San Jose Mercury* and the *San Francisco Chronicle* as being left-wing newspapers. He claimed that the National Guard shot James Rector in self-defense. Reagan stayed about 20 minutes and the repartee degenerated; we talked past each other. When it was over I stood up and could see that he was incredibly made up. I realized that we hadn't been searched and anyone could have killed Reagan on the spot. I had a fantasy that behind the shelves in the room was another head and, if someone killed him, they would just put another head on him and he would go on to meet the next group. It gave me an insight into violence."

When Eugene McCarthy ran for president, Scott helped rent a campaign headquarters in the Common Ground, an old garage across from the town clock in Santa Cruz, California. The town/gown divide was enormous back then, and Scott describes trips to downtown Santa Cruz as "field trips." He helped organize a fast against the war on the steps of the post office and recalls Hal and Barbara Morris from Plaza Books bringing them blankets while others called them names. Some of the students supported Robert Kennedy, who Scott considered an opportunist for not opposing the Vietnam War, but the group ran a highly successful campaign for McCarthy.

Meanwhile Diane, his oldest sister, returned from Uruguay and attended Pacific School of Religion in Berkeley, where she fell in love with James Pike, the retired Episcopal Bishop of California. Pike had already attracted attention for his liberal views; he opposed the war in Vietnam, supported civil rights and women's ordination, and became an outspoken defender of gay rights. In January 1968, Scott drove to Santa Barbara with his parents to visit his sister and meet Pike, who was studying the Dead Sea Scrolls and working on a book about the historic Jesus, set in the context of first century Judaism.

Scott knew enough about the Scrolls to ask Pike questions and when Pike said he was planning a trip to the Middle East, Scott said he'd like to go. Pike encouraged him and, in the spring, Scott left school early to go on a five-week trip with his sister and Pike to visit the historic sites in Jesus' life and to meet with Dead Sea Scroll scholars in Israel, France and England. When they returned, Pike asked Scott to help him with his book and Scott, with the help of Cowell College Provost Page Smith, took the fall semester off.

Bishop Pike and Diane married in December 1968 in August, they returned to the Middle East for their honeymoon. Scott was 21 and traveling across the country to work in a settlement house in Appalachia when he got news that his sister was safe, but Bishop Pike was missing in the

Judean desert.

"Even though I was the youngest, the family sent me to Jerusalem to support my sister, and the last two days I was part of the party searching for Pike's body," said Scott. "We found him on the fifth day. There have been all sorts of speculation about his death, but basically, I think he and my sister were impulsive. They did things no rational person would do. They rented a car and drove into the desert without water, hats, or any supplies. His death totally changed my whole orientation."

When his sister recovered, he returned to Santa Barbara with her and, among her many projects, she insisted on finishing Pike's book, although the book was only ten percent complete. Scott took a break from school to help her despite many interruptions. Bishop Pike had many friends, and everyday "some wacko priest who had lost his job, a shaman, or some guy claiming to be a count from the royal family of Bulgaria," would knock on their door. Scott also accompanied Diane to various venues around the country where she went to fulfill dozens of speaking engagements previously scheduled by Bishop Pike.

The deaths of the students at Kent State upset them so severely that they could no longer work. They decided to move to Jerusalem for six months, where they rented two rooms in a hotel in East Jerusalem. They worked 16- to 18-hour days for three-week stints and then spent five days traveling to Galilee and other areas to visit historic and religious sites. Everyday Scott and Diane would take a bus into West Jerusalem to study Hebrew. Things suddenly changed in September 1970 when the Jordanian civil war began and King Hussein's army crushed Palestinian forces in Jordan's refugee camps.

"We came home one day and the Palestinian Christian family, with whom we were staying, confronted us," Scott said.

"They wanted to know how we, as Christians, could go into West Jerusalem every day and work and study with the Jews who were destroying their family.

Things ripped open. It had been all very civil up to that point, but our relations suddenly became raw during 'Black September.'"

"Nasser died in Egypt. The Palestinians assassinated the Prime Minister of Jordan at Nasser's funeral and started blowing up airplanes. I didn't have a clue as to what was going on. This was a turning point; I turned away from my interest in the historic religious times of Jesus to what was going on around me. I started tracking contemporary affairs and, for thirty years, peace in the Middle East has remained one of my main interests."

After working with James Pike and his sister on the book, Scott was elated to see, *The Wilderness Revolt*, published by Doubleday in 1972, when he was 24. He appreciated being taken seriously by Pike's friends and others, but he found himself becoming impatient with his friends who didn't understand that he wanted to make his own life count for something rather than frittering away his time with trivial distractions.

The university accepted the book as his senior thesis, and he graduated with a major in ancient history, although he spent much less time on campus than the average student. After graduation, one of Pike's friends, William Stringfellow, a lawyer and Episcopal lay theologian, invited Scott to attend a weekend conference, entitled *The Gospel and America*, at the Cathedral of St. John the Divine in New York City.

There he met Dan and Phil Berrigan, "Catholic left" activists against the war.

Scott returned to Isla Vista, near UC Santa Barbara, where he helped organize a similar West Coast conference for the

Christian left, a Catholic Workers Movement in Los Angeles, and others involved in direct action against the war. Scott's views on nonviolent social change were taking shape. After the conference, he and a group of friends decided to remain in Isla Vista.

"In 1973 a bunch of us started a community in Isla Vista that grew to sixteen people," he said. "We started a nonviolence center and met every week to study nonviolence and build a base of support in the community. We experimented with intentional community, and brought films and speakers to the area. We invited a number of influential practitioners of nonviolence to the community: Lanza del Vasto, an Italian who set up a Gandhian Community, The Ark, in France; and Danilo Dolci, an Italian who resisted the Nazis and became a community organizer in Sicily, where he helped to break the Mafia's 'code of silence.'"

In 1974, Scott and Kris were married. She was working on her master's degree and a teaching credential, and Scott informed his draft board that he was going to do his conscientious objector (C.O.) work in Isla Vista. Later that year, a Colonel showed up at his front door to question Scott about the thirty-five C.O.s who were supposed to be working in the area. Scott had never heard of any of them, but as a result, discovered that the draft system was in total disarray.

Most of the men in the Isla Vista group organized projects in the community, while most of the women held jobs on the outside. Although this arrangement worked well for the men, the women decided that Isla Vista was a student ghetto and a terrible place to raise children. The group decided to move and sent out expeditions to locate a more beneficial place to live. Because several members of the group were from UCSC or Northern California, they decided to disband and move to Santa Cruz.

Those interested in an intentional nonviolent community took time off and met in Santa Cruz the following year. In fall 1974, Scott accepted a Rockefeller-sponsored fellowship to study at the Pacific School of Religion in Berkeley. Despite loving Berkeley and the course of study, Scott became disillusioned with the students.

"There were so many people in the seminary who didn't know what they were doing," explained Scott. "I came out of a tradition of Christian activism and, in one class, our assignment was to keep a journal and write about ethical concerns. Some of the students said they couldn't think of anything to write about. I found so much to write about: What about tax resistance? Or driving your car? Or the use of energy resources? Life is full of ethical concerns."

In 1975 Joan Baez asked Scott to become the director of the Institute for the Study of Nonviolence, which she had founded in 1964 in Carmel Valley. The institute moved to Palo Alto when Baez married David Harris, president of the Stanford student body and a leader in the draft resistance movement. Joan asked Scott to become its director because internecine warfare threatened to destroy the institute. He wanted to wait until he finished school in June, but Joan insisted that the situation was grave.

Scott became part-time director, only to find a number of people in the group claimed allegiance to Baez, while others resented her notoriety. When dissenting members presented a list of demands at a board meeting, Scott urged her to accept them. Baez agreed to relinquish control of the institute, but with Baez gone, the opposition lost coherence and the center dissolved. Scott learned some valuable lessons that helped him in creating the Santa Cruz Resource Center for Nonviolence, which received an early boost of monthly support from Baez.

"People only get paid part time and, if we have more

money, we spread it around to more people," explained Scott. "We don't want to create full-time peace bureaucrats and we don't want to become staid and conservative, which happened anyway. Everyone works part time and everyone gets paid the same regardless of how long they work here. We make decisions by consensus and are egalitarian, although it's obvious that someone who has been around for 25 years will have more influence than someone who started more recently. Our values reflect the counter culture and the anti-war movement. Some young people just don't get it; the center grew out of the experiences that shaped us in the Vietnam anti-war and counter-culture movements."

In 1976, at the end of a yearlong hiatus from Isla Vista, eight of the participants formed the nucleus of the Resource Center for Nonviolence in Santa Cruz. The group, which called themselves the Redwood Nonviolence Community, remained together and tithed ten percent of their income. They donated 75 percent of this to various causes and the remainder constituted a loan fund, which helped six of the group's members buy houses, all within a few blocks of each other.

Weekly potlucks brought them together to discuss issues. The Redwood Nonviolence Community continues to meet, although Scott and Kris dropped out in 1999. During this time, Scott and Kris had three children, born in 1976, 1979 and 1982, and continued to live in a house they bought in Santa Cruz in 1976 for $48,000. Kris became a schoolteacher, while Scott stayed home to care for their children and work at the Resource Center. In 1977, the group bought a building at 515 Broadway to house the Resource Center to promote nonviolence and provide a place for the community to gather when political issues convulsed the nation.

Not only does the Center provide a local focus for

promoting peace, but through the years it has also influenced national issues. When the movement against nuclear power plants developed, the Resource Center pushed to include nuclear weapons. Although controversial at first, the two issues are linked today. The Center supported disarmament, and in 1980, qualified a measure for the Santa Cruz County ballot to outlaw the production of parts for nuclear weapons in the county, including the Lockheed plant on Empire Grade. Lockheed spent $240,000 to defeat the measure, while the Campaign for a Nuclear-free Santa Cruz County operated on volunteer labor. Although defeated countywide, Santa Cruz was the first local jurisdiction to use the electoral process to try to ban nuclear weapons and became a model for the nationwide Nuclear Weapons Freeze Movement. The Center participated in demonstrations against the trident missile submarine, Lockheed, and nuclear weapons testing in Nevada.

"Santa Cruz may be a bubble, but we feel we contribute in our own small way to Santa Cruz being what it is," Scott said. "There are fewer nuclear weapons now than at the height of the cold war, but more than we need. We aren't so smart, and we have modest resources, with a staff of 20, but the anti-nuclear weapons movement is mainstream here. We got involved early in the move against intervention in Central America and helped build a network of people — Witness for Peace — to mobilize on the grass roots level against the war in Nicaragua. And we remain interested in peace in the Middle East."

After the Loma Prieta earthquake in 1989, a number of people approached Scott to run for City Council. He resisted at first but his friends argued that his 25 years of participation on national boards such as the War Resisters League, the Fellowship for Reconciliation, Witness for Peace, and the Resource Center for Nonviolence, gave him unique skills. He served on the City Council from 1991 for eight years, one as mayor. After a break imposed by term limits, he returned to the Council in 2001-2003 with a second term as mayor in 2004.

"I've always combined idealism with opportunism and pragmatism," Scott explained. "I don't feel a disruption between my work at the Resource Center and the City Council. The Resource Center draws people who are moralistic and idealistic, and some of them were disappointed when I ran and won. They were disgusted with me participating in government, but I see it as having a synergy with what we're trying to accomplish. Many of the values of the peace movement are well-suited for work on the Council."

Despite criticism, Scott continued to reconcile many sides in disputes within the city. For example, during his first tenure, he concentrated on working with young people and bridging the gap with the Latino population. He fought to curb gang violence and drug use in Beach Flats, as well as to bring much needed street repair and lighting to the area. He supported the filing of multiple small claims against absentee landlords who neglected their property, which led to a $45,000 judgment against them. He remained committed to bringing services to the homeless.

Although some criticized Scott for being too business-friendly and promoting development, he felt that before the earthquake progressive elected officials took business for granted and did nothing to assist this vital part of the community. The two groups, progressives and business people, warily considered each other. When the 1989 earthquake struck and the downtown needed to be rebuilt, Scott helped bring the two warring factions together, playing an important role in resolving conflicts between conservative and progressive forces in Santa Cruz.

"The progressive Santa Cruz leadership has achieved more glory for what it hasn't done than for what it has done," explained Scott. "It prides itself for stopping development of Lighthouse Field and Wilder Ranch. But what about transportation problems? Everyone hates traffic congestion but will we be able to do anything to affect it? After a while people will say we have to do something. While I'm not in favor of widening Highway 1, we have to deal with the railroad corridor and find some creative solutions to our problems. While conservationists say no growth, we have to be aggressive to build affordable housing so people can afford to live here."

Chapter 7: Carmella Weintraub
Saving the Soul of Santa Cruz —
Guidelines for the Preservation of the Character, Historical Qualities and Beauty of Santa Cruz County

It is said that the soul of a place is the sum total of the essence of its highest ideals and should be an expression of its commitment to the good, the true and the beautiful. This quality of soul comes only after the evolution through phases of its development, some of which is challenging and some a natural progress. Then, on both the personality level and the cultural level, integration comes and the soul essence solidifies into a clear and palpable sense of integrity and direction. After facing many changes and challenges in the last 25 years, I feel the soul of Santa Cruz in on the line and I want to respectfully offer my perspective.

I came to Santa Cruz in 1969, the year of the Woodstock Festival, an event that heralded the arrival and growing strength of the counterculture and the beginning of the Aquarian Age. This coincided with my serendipitous landing in a town that seemed on the verge of virtually living the values of that time. I must say, I resonated. The energy here was so positive and real.

The town, which I had known since the 1940's — my great aunt and uncle lived in Paradise Park - had not changed that much since that time. It was still a sleepy little burg, full of senior citizens, retirees in their quaint little one of a kind cottages and students and faculty of the newly minted University and a main drag that sported some nice stores, Leasks and the Morris Abrams store in addition to the Cooper House and numerous small businesses.

I found a city that was bordered on one side by the Pacific Ocean and on the other by giant redwood forests. Between these was a magical strip, which included many charming homes and multiple historic public buildings, built between the Victorian age and the 1950's. In addition, there was a huge amusement part called the Santa Cruz Boardwalk, an iconic symbol of the natural and playful part of human nature. The City on the Hill, the University community, overlooked this whole picture. The arts community, music and entertainment and surfers, boaters and colorful hippies rounded out the palpable spirit of Santa Cruz.

How could one go wrong? Unparalleled pristine beauty, intelligence on the hill and creative energy all around. How could one resist all of that? I moved here. I was 30 years old, give or take a few, and made a life here, knowing this place was special. Finding a job in social services saved me from living on the edge in a place without a huge economic base to support its populace.

The scene blossomed in the 1970's, in the middle of some awesome cultural institutions, both of the Catalysts (old and new), the Cooper House, with live music and dancing by Ginger, Bookshop Santa Cruz, The Teacup Restaurant, the annual Spring Fair and lots and lots of live music groups, art and literary groups. People "owned" the town. Pacific Ave. was turned into the Pacific Garden Mall in 1968 (originally called Downtown Oasis) a plan inspired by Chuck and Esther Abbot.

The mall was basically a non-stop party of music, mirth and exchange of ideas and provided a place where town residents started to mix with University students and their professors, several of whom held forth at the Pergolesi coffee shop behind Bookshop Santa Cruz to lead a weekly forum of the latest ideological point of view. Hanging out at Logos book store was the pastime du Jour. People were out in droves to see and be seen, to enjoy Don McCaslin, the Brothers Karamasov and to enjoy the radically individualistic social scene that was fueled by the general zeitgeist of the times. Tom Noddy, the Bubble Man, even made it to the Johnny Carson show.

It was a fun, unselfconscious time, and even with the advent of recreational drugs, it was still slow, but upbeat, rich and enjoyable, a culture of free spirits, unfettered by the strictures of a culture of conformity.

Perhaps feeding off of some present, but unacknowledged, understanding of what we really had here, social action began to take place in the mid-1970's, focused on preserving the natural settings of Santa Cruz, for all time. During this magnificent period, many Open Spaces were saved for the enjoyment of future generations. Pogonip was saved and annexed by the City in 1978 and would not be developed for housing. In 1974, a committed group of Santa Cruz citizens organized to keep Wilder Ranch from the ravages of north coast development. Later, in 1978, Lighthouse Point was saved, also from development, and later converted to a State Park, a status which endures until now providing perhaps the most beloved gathering spot in our city. Even later in the '70s Arana Gulch became a permanent greenbelt and would remain committed to its pristine original nature- green, wet and wild.

Money was beginning to creep into the culture of Santa Cruz, but not in a greedy or ostentatious way. Houses on Westcliff were sold and other large ones built but still, there was the original feeling of Santa Cruz. A place for many people, visitors and residents alike to enjoy a place of rest, rejuvenation, relaxation and renewal. It was a magical time and things were about to change dramatically.

At the end of the 1980's, there occurred a sudden and major shift. The Loma Prieta earthquake hit, decimating the Pacific Garden Mall and killing 3 people. I was downtown with my young children at the time and witnessed this tragic event. The damage was so extensive that the Mall lost its Historic status because 19 of 36 buildings that qualified for the appellation just two years prior to the quake were lost. Future generations would never see the examples of 1890s to 1929 architecture. The Cooper House, deemed unsafe by City officials, came down, despite the protests of hundreds of tearful onlookers.

This loss was a metaphor for much more that was lost in the Earthquake because in the ensuing years many aspects of Santa Cruz changed. In the nanoseconds following the earthquake, the town was plunged into a crisis of major proportions. The town was in shambles and soon so was the spirit of Santa Cruz. We had lost our center.

Very quickly, outside professional urban planning consultants were called in to consult on what our town should look like, despite their lack of familiarity as to what the DNA of Santa Cruz had always been. Our hip little town soon became a "chic" little town and started a trend that was to continue until this very day.

After the earthquake the local ambience and architecture changed very rapidly and often surprisingly with less public input than was probably fair. Costco, our first city big box store, opened in 1994. A few years later, in a sudden departure from our historic heritage, Gateway Center opened in 1997, much to the chagrin of the small business owners who had their charming and historic buildings knocked down. Replacing these historic businesses with what turned out to be a strip mall in the shape of a square, housing businesses at the gateway to our town, in non-descript box like stores with no apparent nod to the look and feel of our town. As if that were not enough shock. Soon modern design, coupled with a garish green paint on metal standards, appeared in the form of lighting on River St., ostensibly to create a welcoming look to the historic center of town. In the opinion of many citizens, this goal was never achieved.

There were many shocked people, including myself, but as local architect — activist Mark Primack stated, at the time, after only two people showed up at the design review planning meetings, "the citizens of Santa Cruz will get what they deserve". I am recalling all of this because I believe we are at a similar juncture now. If we don't get actively involved in setting the course of development in this town, we will again be the recipients of something we do not want nor deserve.

After this particular surprise, more change came about and currently continues to come about, fast and furiously as the City fathers (and mothers) move quickly to fill in every empty space in Santa Cruz city limits with high density potentially generically designed "infill", a phenomenon that is currently in process now, led by the Santa Cruz City Council and City Planners.

To that end, currently on the table or in process are these projects:

The Corridor Plan, putting high density, tall buildings and hotels on Ocean St. Soquel Ave, Water St. and Mission St.

The Active Transportation Plan, a plan containing 260 separate projects all over the city to encourage bicycle and walking transportation and safety. Some of the projects disturb neighborhood unity, safety and aesthetics with signage and changes the neighborhood residents do not want to see in their established places of habitation. Other projects invite unbidden crime to enter quiet neighborhoods that are particularly vulnerable.

The Wharf Plan, potentially putting high density, tall buildings on the wharf, creating issues in congestion, questionable aesthetics and future dangers if sea levels do rise,

The Hyatt hotel in place of the former Unity Church, out of place in this particular crowded neighborhood with congested streets.

Potentially moving the present downtown City Library to the space displacing the Farmer's Market and putting in a multilevel parking garage where none currently exists, at that site.

Increased non-aesthetic designs (so far) on the planned San Lorenzo River high-end housing development. No plan for controlling aesthetics.

Increased development of the tech industry coupled with high speed Internet cable.

Destruction of more historical housing and buildings, especially on high profile streets.

More freeway lanes going to and from Watsonville, yielding more pollution and greenhouse gases. Coming in 2021.

Private development of housing that does not meet the economic needs of most local citizens, low income and homeless populations.

Allowing cell phone towers all over our county on public right of ways. Verizon leased from Crown Castle, all private corporations.

Why is this all-important and where are we going with this? And why? What can we do?

Taken together and followed by potentially more changes, these planned projects would change the face of our city in radical ways. We need to determine our personal response to these intended changes and act on our convictions on behalf of all stakeholders, including visitors and future children. We need, as a community, to take stock of exactly what values we hold dear and exactly what we are losing by not honoring these values.

First, let's be clear, these concerns are not about maintaining the status quo or about nostalgia. They are about maintaining our spiritual, aesthetic and moral center in the face of an increasingly inhuman environment which is killing people and compromising the sanity of many of our citizens, young and old and obliterating natural resources and open space.

There are many practical issues associated with planned changes for Santa Cruz, many of which are long-term concerns. First, can the infrastructure we have now support new development, especially those that will house many residents or visitors? Currently, our infrastructure of roads, sidewalks and buildings need repairing before money is spent on private development. Secondly and importantly, can we continue to supply water and other resources to new development and still service existing citizens? While new hotels can support the sagging tax base, the concern that current water users have is valid. We have contributed here for years. Thirdly, why are taxes not levied on the multi-million dollar homes that are being built? The alternative, sales tax, creates an overdependence on materialism and shopping. Fourthly, how are all economic levels of citizens going to be able to remain here to enliven the mix of cultures and points of view we have historically enjoyed?

These are all valid, reality-based concerns for our citizens but there are also meta-issues which cannot be addressed at town hall meetings and these involve concerns that are often talked about in private conversations and they affect a large constituency of residents, visitors and future generations of same. Let me express, as a longterm resident of this town, how I experience the many hidden values of our town and what we can do to save these before it is too late.

I feel Santa Cruz (Holy Cross) is a sanctuary, a holy sacred space for all who venture into these environs. The operative word here is ALL. Over the years, we have developed something special here and Santa Cruz' charm and values are a magnet for people all over the United States and the world as well. I submit that Santa Cruz is a center of counter culture for a reason and is known worldwide for the way we live. As our mainstream culture speeds up, creates crowded, concrete communities overloaded with technology and cars and speed, we have maintained a commitment to something slower, saner and unique. It is perhaps a one-of-a-kind experience. Indeed, Santa Cruz IS an experience, a state of mind that is almost indescribable. We have much to offer a world-weary population and we must adhere to the core values and the gifts we offer to the planet. And they are many. Our human lives actually rely on the necessity of regeneration, relaxation, recreation and rest. Our nervous systems actually demand this and the price we pay for not adhering to these necessities is illness, sometimes severe and often expressed as continuing low grade stress.

We have many healers here and it is, in my opinion, because we are a healing community. People need what we have, all people. We must remain faithful to the part we play in healing the homeless, the frazzled, the young and the restless and let's not forget our seniors, the original inhabitants of this retirement community. We owe this to them as well as our children and future generations.

The chance to experience nature at its finest on miles of currently protected beaches and hundreds of square miles of redwood forests is priceless and nurturing and is, in essence, the basis of our healing atmosphere. The pace in Santa Cruz is not syncopated or staccato but, instead, more lyrical and softly entrained to the rhythm of the ocean and its playful inhabitant creatures. This is our DNA. Nature is our "brand" and in keeping with that, countless human beings can remain a natural human and even more can come here and remember what it is to be fully human. Through the enjoyment of our natural resources, we can experience the joyful and natural state that is evoked by our beautiful beaches and the countless other recreational opportunities that our environment offers.

In a time when cultural mania is increasing to megalomania and the metropolis becomes megalopolis; we have an example, here, of how to balance this trend. Hyperactivity is a national illness and it is up to us to remain a clear beacon for an alternative way to live. Indeed, Santa Cruz has the ability to provide an active model for a viable life-style alternative. A lot is riding on our commitment to modeling how it is to be fully human, related to nature, to each other and our fellow inhabitants of the planet. In these meta-respects, we are a model city.

Coupled with our natural resources, our University culture and our small, human size homes and public buildings, each with its individual look, we have created a culture of connected individualism, environmental sanity and ecological consciousness. Artists, musicians, creators, imaginers, young and old, people of diverse orientations, rich and poor, come together to create a culture of character and diversity which is unmatched anywhere. Why would we want to ruin this by importing any of the insanity that is what ruins most other large communities. To do so would, in and of itself, be insanity of the highest order.

We should not become a Silicon Beach. We do not need to be a bedroom community of Silicon Valley and we do not necessarily need to grow. We should not become Monterey and we are not Carmel with its quaint arts community. We simply need to continue to be ourselves and honor what has come to be an amazing place centered as we are on the edge of the Pacific Rim.

I believe we are here with a spiritual charge to balance the insanity of the techno, bureaucratic, corporate industrial complex. With the protection of the forest on one side and the sea on the other, we are a virtual island of sanity. We are a true oasis of intelligence and creation and beacon of individual freedom to each be who we are as essence and to also share in the rich and diverse community that we share. We must do what we can to retain the paradise that we have. In the spirit of dialogue, I humbly offer the following suggestions to perhaps stimulate a discussion about how we can help maintain a commitment to existing beauty and value in this town,.

OUR TASKS

Support activities and leaders who will not gentrify, technologize, monetize or materialize (nor caffeinate) our community nor exploit human or natural resources to these ends.

Support the continuance of spiritual development and higher consciousness here, thus encouraging each individual to reach his or her full potential.

Support spontaneous grass roots level creativity, especially collaborative kinds of projects and events for all ages and stages of life..

Support those activities which do not exploit our natural and historic collective resources on behalf of a few, whether that is government, private citizens or outside developers.

Support aesthetic building and public art and design which is in keeping with our historic legacy. This entails keeping the landscape "low rise" as opposed to high rise.

Support those policies which do not allow crowding out the citizens of this area who are operating in the lower socio-economic levels.

Support those changes which do not increase speed, concrete, cars or exclusive money. Economic development must be based on values of economic moderation and inclusiveness of all levels.

Support activities, people and policies that allow us to keep our natural rhythm, size and connectivity. Choose that which supports harmony, diversity, inclusiveness and diversity.

Support the development of a process for ongoing public input and voting on each proposed development that has the capacity to change the DNA of our community. Encourage referendum process.

Support density in what is already here, change zoning laws to allow development of the many small outbuildings that abound in the city of Santa Cruz.

Support individuals to accept responsibility and accountability for the role he or she plays in the evolution of our planet and indeed, our very existence.

This includes responsibility for not over-populating the planet, for not condoning any form of violence or brutality and for respecting all beings as worthy of dignity and acceptance.

We need to unify our energies and goals for this town and listen closely to every voice. The planet and we have a lot at stake. It is not too late to save what we have created in this village by the sea. We are capable of leading the nation in propagating values that lead to quality human lives as well as the other kingdoms with whom we share the planet, lives unburdened by values not developed in our true interests- that of being happy, healthy and connected with our whole planet and Universe.

Lastly, it is important that we elect leaders who understand the language of the soul. This means making collaborative decisions and working through a channel of what feels right, not only what a few think is right. Leaders need to listen carefully to all citizens who choose to speak up and it is my feeling that it needs to be longer than 2 or 3 minutes per speaker (as it currently stands in the City Council). Santa Cruz people know the language of the soul and we need to speak up on behalf of what we might lose if we don' t make our values known. We have way too much to lose if we stay silent. Many citizens, present and future are depending on us to serve the highest good of all.

Chapter 8: Ralph Abraham
David Theirmann Interview

RA: September 4, 2018 and I'm here at home with David Theirmann. David, I looked back over the tapes that you did interviewing me, I think it was 25-30 years ago, and there were eight hours all together. Here if we try to cover the same ground in an hour, it will have to be carefully done. So I thought I would start with your childhood, and then maybe fast forward up to the time you came to Santa Cruz. Most of the interviews in the past, I've asked the person to start with their arriving in Santa Cruz, but I'm very interested in the question of how you got to be the person that you are, so maybe you can start with where you were born in your family and your early childhood and stuff.

DT: Yeah, so I was conceived in New Jersey, and I was born in Philadelphia in 1946, and my parents were Quakers, and my father was working for the American Friends Service Committee, which is an interdenominational, nonsectarian service organization for the Quakers, and my uncle was also working for them, so it was a big influence on my life.

RA: This was in Philadelphia.

DT: That's where their headquarters are. And I lived in Chicago slums for about a year or two while my father was working on rehabilitating some apartments there for black people. And then we moved to Santa Monica, and I grew up in Santa Monica, and my uncle continued to work for the American Friends Service Committee. He was running the Northern California division out of San Francisco. And then he went on to become their representative to the United Nations, and also handled all their diplomats when he was living in Geneva for many years. So there was that influence with the family. And my father, as I was growing up, had a tree surgery company in West Los Angeles, but his real love was being involved with this service organization, as an activist.

RA: What does a service organization usually do?

DT: Well they have all sorts of projects all over the world to help people, to be of service. As an example, as I was growing up, I had the opportunity to work on a number of different Indian reservations, when I was a teenager: Pala Indian Reservation, Morongo Indian Reservation — these were like summer work camps with other young people. And then I had the opportunity to go with a group of teenagers to Ciudad Victoria, on the east coast of Mexico, to help refurbish a church there, as a summer project. And then I went to Canada to help build a school in British Columbia. So that was a big influence on my life.

RA: And these were all projects of the American Friends Service organization?

DT: Yes, the American Friends Service Committee. It won the Nobel Prize for Peace during World War I, and so they had a good reputation. And then, as I got older, I had the opportunity to also go on a project in Haïti in the Caribbean, helping to rebuild a public health dispensary, and then I was three years in East Africa, in Tanzania in the southern highlands, working in a Lepertarium, otherwise known as a Hanson's Disease Hospital.

RA: This was in your high school years?

DT: That was in my college years.

RA: I see.

DT: I was doing alternative service as a conscientious objector at that point. That was from 1965 through 1968. I had started off at UC Berkeley in '63. Transferred to UC Santa Barbara in '65, and then went to Africa for three years doing my alternative service as a conscientious objector, and that's when I was working at the Lepertarium for three years, and that was also sponsored by the American Friends Service Committee. My job there was to provide a thousand patients in the hospital with a means of employment in occupational therapy, and I did that by starting a business making traditional African musical instruments and artifacts. And so it was a lot of fun and I learned a lot. This was in Tanzania at the Lepertarium. And then when I came back from that, I came to UC Santa Cruz in '69, and luckily they had the Merrill Field Program, which allowed me to get 30 units retroactive credit for the three years I'd worked in the hospital in Tanzania, and they also allowed me to get 10 units of credit for studying Afro-Haitian musical instruments connected with Voodoo ceremonies in Haiti, and 15 units for organizing a TV series in Brazil for the Ministry of Health, about public health education. So I actually graduated from UC Santa Cruz in 1971, and I graduated in the Amazon. That was my last 15 units of credit. And then I traveled all over South America with another UCSC student. She was collecting pre-Colombian textiles and I was collecting musical instruments. So we hit all of the festivals and all the museums in every country in South America except Venezuela, and that took about a year to do that. And I came back to Santa Cruz in '72.

RA: That was your whole college program, in fact. You've hardly mentioned a course. It was all these field experiences.

DT: I ended up getting a degree in African Studies, and thanks to the field program at UC Santa Cruz, it was a very valuable education for me. I do a lot better in the field than I do in a classroom. That's my style.

RA: So you came to UCSC in '69 and then you graduated in '71. And then did you stay in Santa Cruz after that?

DT: When I came back from South America, I tried a stint at UC Berkeley in a graduate program of public health education, but it wasn't my cup of tea, so I took a leave of absence in '72 and came back to Santa Cruz, and I was very upset coming back to Santa Cruz, because I had no idea what I was going to be doing next. A friend, who had been renting a home in Scotts Valley, made the mistake of trying to turn a closet inside of the home into a sauna by building a wood-burning stove inside the closet, and he burned the house down, and all he had left was an old Ford pickup truck and a pair of boots. His father felt sorry for him and gave him enough money to drive down to L.A. to buy two tons of oranges for three cents a pound and haul them up in a trailer, and he was trying to sell them for ten cents a pound in the local flea market in Santa Cruz, and he was unable to sell them fast enough and they were going rotten, and that's why he called me and asked me if I'd be willing to come and help him, and initially I didn't want to do it because I was afraid one of my former professors at UC Santa Cruz might see me at the flea market selling oranges, but then I thought about it for a while and I didn't have a plan, so I decided to go out there and sell oranges with him, and we were having a lot of fun selling them by the 10-pound sack. We moved all the oranges, and then we bought four tons from the packing houses and went door to door in Santa Cruz. It took sixteen months. We knocked on every door in Santa Cruz County, selling oranges by handing out samples by the box. We would buy them for ten dollars a box and sell them for twenty. And we needed a place to store the produce, because now we were buying eight tons of oranges at a time, so someone by the name of Richard Alderson rented us, for fifty bucks a month, an old VW garage on North Pacific Avenue, across from the town clock, up against the cliffs there. The Crepe Place used to be at one end, and then there was United Bar, and Indian Ambrosia, and then there was our place, where we were storing produce, and then Bodhi Dharma's, which was a coffee and tea shop on the other side. We had no intention of using the space other than to store the produce, because —

RA: Are we in 1972 still?

DT: This was in 1974. But one thing led to another, and at night we were in there, and we bought a blender, and we were playing music and making smoothies for our friends, and by the end of four years we had 30 employees and we were doing stuffed cornish game hens and trout stuffed with shrimp, and we had an open stage for anyone to perform from 10 in the morning until midnight, seven days a week. I never auditioned anyone, so all the slots were taken. We had mime, belly dancing, juggling, fire eating, sword swallowing, lectures on every type of subject, every type of musical instrument. So it was a lot of fun. This was called the Good Fruit Company.

RA: I remember that.

DT: I sold that in 1979, and went to French Polynesia, to do research about French Polynesian musical instruments, because I found out that the musical instruments in French Polynesia are identical to the ones I found in the Amazon when I was working in Brazil. So I came back after that and went back to selling oranges again, but this time I went door to door, and I only did office spaces in Santa Cruz County. So I went into every office space in Santa Cruz County, from Boulder Creek to Aptos, with a box of free oranges and a knife, and I'd hand out samples to people in the office spaces, and they would buy them from the box from me. And I did that for a number of years, until I got burned out, and one of my customers, who was selling ceramics, noticed that I was getting burned out, and she felt sorry for me, and she said that she had a trade with a career counselor that she wasn't going to use. And she gave that to me, and I met this guy in a coffee shop. He was a career counselor, and he took some notes on me as I was talking about my career for about an hour, and I walked out of the coffee shop and I thought: That was kind of fun. Maybe I'll be a career counselor. That was 1987, and 31 years later, I'm still a career counselor.

RA: You settled down.

DT: I settled down. I meet people all over Santa Cruz County, in every coffee shop and every restaurant, to talk about their lives, and —

RA: Where do they find you?

DT: They find me by either looking for me on Yelp, or they find me by looking for me on Google, or they see my advertisement in the Good Times, or they see stories that have been written about me in the newspapers, or they get referred to me by other clients. So I have had about 4,000 people that I've had the privilege of getting to know over the last thirty years, and they were all very, very open to telling me their life story. And we go all the way back to their grandparents, and notice how all those relatives affect them genetically and environmentally to be who they are, and then we go through their entire life, all the way up to their death, as though they were dead looking back over their life, to check out the parameters of their imagination. If they can't imagine this happening, it's probably not going to happen. Of all the surveys and tests that I give my career-counselor clients, I'd say that's the most fun part, to hear their story. Because everybody's got a story to tell.

RA: So people, after talking to you, then they sometimes have a transformation, I suppose? I mean they come to see you because they want to change?

DT: That's correct, and they either come to me because they're unclear as to what direction they want to go with their lives. If that's the case, then I'll give them surveys and tests and the biographical inventory to access their capabilities and confidence levels and motivations and values, so we can get real clear as to what would be appropriate for them. Or, they come to me because they're already focused like a laser beam on their direction, and they don't need the clarity, they just want to develop their ideas or their dreams or their thoughts. If that's the case, we work on their marketing skills or their management skills or their business skills or their networking skills to develop their ideas.

RA: So typically a client comes to you for multiple visits.

DT: Some of my clients have been with me for years. We'll meet once a week or once a month, and other clients I only see them maybe once and I never see them again.

RA: Backing up a little bit, can you tell me about your siblings. I mean, growing up you had brothers and sisters?

DT: I'm the oldest. I have a brother, Eric, who has a video production company in Santa Cruz called ImpactCreative.com, and he travels all over the world doing documentaries and corporate videos, promotional videos. And I also have a sister, Anne, who teaches art at UC Extension and Cabrillo College and Monterey Peninsula College, and she plays the organ for one of the local churches. And then I have two other half sisters who live in L.A., and one works for an architect and the other one works for an attorney.

RA: So Eric and Anne settled in Santa Cruz after you did, or before?

DT: Actually, before. My brother Eric came to Santa Cruz the first year UC Santa Cruz opened up in 1965.

RA: He's a pioneer student.

DT: A pioneer student. And the university needed someone to document the growth of the university, and so he volunteered. They gave him a Pentax camera and unlimited film, and he shot hundreds of thousands of photographs of the university as it developed, from 1965 until he graduated and went on to get his masters in film at UCLA. My sister Anne transferred in from Mills College in Oakland, and became a Cowell student. My brother was also a Cowell student. I was a Merrill student. And so all three of us wound up at UC Santa Cruz, and what's kind of interesting is, we all ended up becoming documentarians. I document by actually writing down notes that I take while people are talking. My brother documents with video. And my sister documents by doing murals or paintings. And it's kind of curious to me that we all ended up as documentarians.

RA: So do you see them regularly now? I suppose you do.

DT: We don't see each other that often unless it's a celebration or a birthday party or something like that. In order to stay in touch with each other, we try to get together at my sister's place once a month to have breakfast, just to stay connected.

RA: Excellent. So you've got a way of life that suits you as a life, and also a profession, so that it seems unlikely that you'll change to some other future career.

DT: Yeah, it looks like I'm going to be sticking with this particular career until I retire, but I don't have any plans to retire at this point. I'll be 73 in January. And I feel very fortunate over the years that I had the opportunity to have four thousand students — four thousand professors, who were my clients, teaching me, and getting paid to be the student. I was their student and they were my professors.

RA: Have you given any thought to creating a document or any kind of combination of your experiences from the four thousand professors, a distillation of the ideas that you've learned?

DT: I've had ideas about that. I have a storage container that houses the four thousand documents. Some of them are over a thousand pages long. And I haven't figured out yet exactly how I would take all of those documents and put them into something that would be valuable for people. Plus it's all confidential information.

RA: What you've learned is like a distillation of a distillation of all that material down to a level where there are certain principles or ideas about life, or lessons or something, that you could only export from your own mind, quite independent of all this recorded material from four thousand stories, because there are similarities in the stories, and some stories reinforce ideas you got from another one and so on. So by now, your wisdom is a kind of a blessing.

DT: One thought I had at some point, I was thinking about what is the most popular book — or one of the most popular books in the world, and it happens to be a book called The Bible. And the Bible is an accumulation of stories that people put together of what was happening to them, generation after generation, and it was passed down, so I've fantasized what it would be like if there was some way to take these four thousand files and somehow put them together as *The Bible According to David Thiermann* or something like that, to share with people.

RA: You could fictionalize a little bit, and combine certain real characters into a fictitious combination, and tell that story. The Bible actually has these stories covering generations, but there are only a few stories, and the actual input that created that distilled wisdom must be four thousand or forty thousand stories, that distillation process happened in your mind, and I think that it would be so valuable to have a way to recount that for people.

DT: I'm very open to collaborating with anyone that might be interested in utilizing the material to create something that would be helpful for people.

RA: Well I think the person to collaborate with is you. You mentioned retirement, so do you have a date in mind —

DT: I do not have a date in mind. For me personally, I need a lot of fellowship, and so that's probably the reason why I'm in this profession, because it allows me to have an intimate relationship with a lot of different people.

RA: You can't retire.

DT: It's a need that I have. One of the things that happened that I didn't mention earlier, was that before I started this current career counseling business, I had the opportunity in 1983 to be the first ambassador of an organization called Conflict Limited, in Santa Cruz. It was started by a professor of peace studies at Merrill College, Earl Reynolds, He and his wife had been living in Hiroshima for many years, and they asked me if I would be willing to be their ambassador to Hiroshima for a year. And so I had the opportunity to live in Hiroshima for a year, in 1983, and it allowed me to go to a lot of Sumo wrestling, traditional tea ceremonies, museums, temples, schools, factories, and live with about 30 different Japanese families. So it was a very valuable experience. And it was attempting to improve business relations between Japanese and American businessmen. I forgot to mention that when you had asked me what happened, chronologically.

RA: Well you might be missing the international aspect of your life. Do you do much traveling now?

DT: I don't. And I'm still very fortunate that I did a lot of my traveling when I was much younger and had a lot more idealism and naiveté and testosterone. Because in a way I feel like those are all three important things that helped me be so adventuresome in that point in my life. But the motivation or the ambition to do the kind of traveling that I did back then isn't as great.

RA: Traveling gets more and more difficult with each passing year. Well there might be, besides writing "the bible," some alternative for sharing your accumulated wisdom with people locally by doing a series of talks or some kind of informal course in the alternative college or something.

DT: When I'm with a client, if they're open to it, I'm happy to share my experiences with them on an individual basis, in addition to encouraging them to share their experiences with me, so it's an exchange in that way, on both sides. I take notes on everything they say, in detail, and then I feed that information back to them at the beginning of the next session, just to make sure I got the information correct, and many of the clients feel that it's very therapeutic to be able to externalize their thoughts and their feelings, and have it documented, so —

RA: And you're seeing several people in one week, sometimes more than one in a day?

DT: At the peak of my career consulting business, there were days where I would see seven or eight people in one day. But I found that I would be a basket case for the next two days if I tried to book that many people into one day. And now I find that I can't really handle more than three or four hours a day of clients, because it's an intense experience, and, so I have to pace myself.

RA: You begin repeat sessions with a client with a resume of the previous meeting, you have to do some homework before you meet with that person, there has to be an interval between one client and another, in order to do that.

DT: I feel very blessed to be able to take notes while someone's talking, because I'm working with so many different people at the same time, if I didn't take detailed notes, after a while it would all become one big vegetable soup and I wouldn't remember who said what. But because it's all documented, I can read back over it, and clear it with the client, find out if indeed that's what they said, so that we can analyze it and take a closer look at what they're really trying to say.

RA: You must be very, very expert at note-taking.

DT: When people look at my handwriting, they usually look at it upside-down, because I'm sitting across from them, and many of them will say, "Are you a doctor?" and the reason they say that is that my handwriting at this point is completely illegible as you can tell from looking at it, and it used to be pretty legible, when I first started writing thirty years ago, but for some reason, I'm getting more creative with my handwriting over time.

Chapter 9: Rick Alan
Out of the Haze —
How a Hip Burg by the Edge of the Sea
Turned-On the World.

Though it's not a generally well-known story, a Hip History of Santa Cruz would be missing a key chapter without a look at the birth and spread of "Connoisseur Cannabis" at the tail end of the sixties. It was a veritable horticultural revolution that drafted on the winds of hip culture's sea-change and eventually grandparented today's complex Connoisseur Cannabis market, medical marijuana industry and state-by-state legalization movements that defy ossified federal policies of criminalization that are, despite entrenched resistance of the carceral state, inevitably eroding away.

The various accounts that exist of this revolution in pot breeding and cultivation are sketchy, anecdotal and somewhat awash in disputed details, and as is often the case of topics that treat the history of outlawed, if not demonized activities, they are found to dwell off the beaten path. On the other hand, now that marijuana is gaining legal status around the country and shedding its "demon rum" shamefulness in the eyes of straight society, the dark days of heavy criminalization are beginning to recede and pioneering tales of the modern pot culture are stepping out of the shadows. Only beginning though, for just as several federal level decriminalization bills have sprouted up in congress recently, heavy reactionary interests from big pharma and the puritanical right are digging in their heals — think Trump's DOJ.

Those shadows are long, dark and tragic indeed and most Hip History readers probably know the litany well. The use of anti-marijuana laws as a means of repression and control via decades of police harassment and racially lopsided mass incarceration is common knowledge. The imprisonment of so many hundreds of thousands of people, mostly people of color, for possession, distribution or personal use of pot far dwarfs those jailed for all violent crimes combined. The initiation of the "War on Drugs" by the Nixon administration was a thinly veiled attempt to suppress the perceived threat of domestic revolutionary political and cultural activity.

So let's take a moment to review the story of cannabis use in this country and the events that led to the criminalizing of marijuana, the doubling down of recreational drug-use repression and the simultaneous emergence of designer, or "connoisseur cannabis".

The material, pharmaceutical and psychoactive properties of various species of cannabis have been known in human culture for at least twelve thousand or more years. The plant itself is believed to have been cultivated originally in the steppes of Central Asia during the Neolithic period. Its psychoactive qualities are first noted in the historical record in China during the third millennium B.C. and use was widespread in Europe long before colonization of the New World. The Spanish brought hemp, a particularly fast-growing variety of Cannabis sativa, to the Western Hemisphere and cultivated it in Chile in the 1540s, and Wampanoag natives were reported harvesting wild-growing hemp around Cape Cod in 1605.

Growing hemp in the early period of our nations history was common and perfectly legal. Its fiber and seeds were used for an astonishing variety of purposes and was a cash crop for many big landowners during colonial times, including the big Kahuna, George Washington, as well as at least a half-dozen succeeding presidents. By 1890 it had replaced cotton as the main cash crop of the southern states. As early as the 1830's hemp, in addition to uses of its fiber for rope, fabric and clothing (the word canvas comes from cannabis) and the oil from its seeds, was commonly used to treat a wide variety of medical ailments. By the turn of the 19th century a majority of over-the-counter and prescription pharmaceuticals contained extracts of cannabis and cocaine, as well as opium. This last point is important for two reasons: the first anti-drug law in the country, put on the books ironically in San Francisco in 1875, outlawed opium smoking and was aimed at the Chinese community, leading to arrests and deportations; and secondly, later anti-marijuana laws were modeled on this act. Additionally, in a stone-cold foreshadow of the racist, 100-1 sentencing disparity between crack and powdered cocaine possession during the abominable War on Drugs (1970-2010, which especially victimized the black community), when opium smoking was made a federal offense in 1909 the law excluded drinking and injecting tincture of opium, popular among the white population.

Starting roughly with the Mexican Revolution in 1910, immigration into the U.S. from south of the border began to swell and people brought along a form of cannabis which had been used in their culture for centuries, not only medicinally but also, unlike in the U.S., recreationally. Americans had cannabis in their medicines but these immigrants smoked "marijuana" and jingo politicians in Louisiana and Texas, along with fevered media accounts of the "marijuana menace" promoted searching for pot at the border as the preferred excuse to detain and deport Mexicans. The anti-Mexican immigrant drumbeat continued for a couple of decades, associating its use with "killers, drug addicts, criminals," etc. (sound familiar?).

Between 1916 and 1930 twenty-nine states outlawed marijuana. In 1930 the Treasury Department opened a new division — the Federal Bureau of Narcotics — and put zealot

Henry Anslinger in charge. The FBN immediately went batshit loony, lumping marijuana in with cocaine and heroin and blasting out such outrageous and racist claims as:

"There are 100,000 total marijuana smokers in the US, and most are Negroes, Hispanics, Filipinos, and entertainers. Their satanic music, jazz, and swing, result from marijuana use. This marijuana causes white women to seek sexual relations with Negroes, entertainers, and any others."

"The primary reason to outlaw marijuana is its effect on the degenerate races." (You think they meant white women and people of color?)

"Marijuana is an addictive drug which produces in its users insanity, criminality, and death."

"Reefer makes darkies think they're as good as white men."

"Marihuana leads to pacifism and communist brainwashing"

"You smoke a joint and you're likely to kill your brother."

"Marijuana is the most violence-causing drug in the history of mankind."

(From "The Racist roots of Marijuana Prohibition; by David McDonald; The Foundation for Economic Education)

The hysterical press magnate W.R. Hearst sold papers with steamy stories of Mexican mayhem and generally used his bully pulpit to defend his vast lumber/paper mill holdings against the hemp industry. Pharmaceutical and chemical companies, such as DuPont jumped in for obvious reasons. In 1935 F.D.R. gave props to Anslinger. In 1936 the movie "Reefer Madness" was released, warning distraught parents that drug-dealing criminals would lure their kids to "jazz parties" and get them hooked on reef. Congress decided it had to do something to protect the virtue of America and all this political and economic clout culminated in the Marijuana Tax Act of 1937, and the federal war on marijuana had officially begun.

The courts finally overturned the MTA in 1969 on Fifth Amendment grounds. [Btw: The AMA had always opposed the MTA, which led to the semi-legalizing of marijuana for medical purposes]. But then Congress immediately passed the Controlled Substances Act in 1970 with its "schedules" of relative addictiveness. The most restrictive category — Schedule I, lumps marijuana in with the obvious heroin but then includes a strange, and in some cases ridiculous group of others including Quaaludes, MDMA (Ecstasy), DMT, LSD, Peyote, Psilocybin and Mescaline, demonstrating a clear bias against psychoactive substances. The less restricted II category includes: amphetamine, cocaine, barbiturates, codeine, methamphetamine, oxycodone, morphine, etc. You get the picture. The Shafer Commission, which advised congress during creation of the bill, had actually recommended the decriminalization of pot, but to no avail.

The feds have clung doggedly to their rationalizations for criminalizing marijuana and characterizing it as among the most addictive and dangerous of substances, against overwhelming evidence to the contrary, and over the objections of the AMA, innumerable scientific studies, legal and law-enforcement organizations, and plain old good sense. The damage created by treating drug use as a moral/legal question as opposed to a health issue is in many ways incalculable, ruining countless lives and causing more misery than any possible misuse of drugs ever could. The states have begun to recognize this, thankfully, and perhaps federal decimalization, at least of marijuana, is somewhere on the horizon. But the issue concerning the racist roots of these laws and their usefulness to the corporate state as tools of social control, e.g. the connection to the prison industry, remains deeply disturbing.

Meanwhile, back in the Cruz:

Santa Cruz, with its surfer sub-culture and satellite status in the San Francisco/Big Sur, Bohemian/Beatnik/Hippie nexus, has long had a marijuana profile. The proximity to a Mexican-American community via south county agriculture around Watsonville and environs, as well as the well-beaten path of surfing safaris down the coast to Mexico and Baja has always provided access to regular old "mota". The scene began to transition in the late sixties from a staple of generally uninspiring Mexican "reg", such as the old standbys of Oxacan, Michoacan, and Guerrero Green. These varieties were found virtually everywhere people distributed and smoked the stuff, including UCSC and it's surging population of mostly middle-class, young quasi-hipsters on the hill.

It usually arrived here smuggled into the states from Mexico by intrepid outlaws risking serious jail time, in a variety of cars, trucks and airplanes. Returning vets from Vietnam, with newly acquired single and double prop craft flying skills bumped the traffic up a significant notch. Pressed into kilogram "bricks" (2.2 lbs. for the metrically challenged), the low-rent contraband quickly filtered out into the community of anxious stoners because everybody knew that — in the words of cartoonist Gilbert Shelton's "Fabulous Furry Freak Brothers" — "*Dope* will *get you through times of no money better than money will get you through times* of *no dope.*" It was pretty much low-grade in potency, having been grown in rural areas by small farmers, hidden among rows of corn, harvested crudely, and when plopped on the kitchen table by an end user who had "scored" a twenty-five dollar, one-ounce "lid", it was quickly sifted and cleaned of the inevitable, unsmokeable "seeds and stems", ritually rolled into joints and happily lit up for an evening (or morning) toke. Despite the endless hysterical rants of the morality police, it was well known among the user community that pot wasn't a "gateway drug". I know more hippies who went on to become real-estate agents than eternally damned indigents. And, in the following years, if you placed all the established — if not downright respectable — businesses that bootstrapped their initial financing from dealing a little boo, you could probably create a gentrified neighborhood.

By the late sixties better stuff from more distant and exotic locales began appearing around town. Smugglers were ramping up the ante right when the feds were cracking down and beginning to "weaponize" police departments in order to tighten domestic surveillance and control. The Black Panthers, Brown Berets and Weatherpersons were perceived as such palpable threats that law-enforcement was losing track of the new import vectors for weed from places like Thailand, Hawaii, South Africa, Panama and Columbia. In addition to the venerable "Acapulco Gold" — the old standby, go-to status smoke for flush locals — there were much higher potency, better tasting and sweeter smelling types such as Thai-stick, Kona Gold, Maui Wowie, Panama and Columbian Red and the especially intriguing Durban Poison available in the marketplace and in demand by those with an actual sustainable income. And what's more, the idea of growing your own, a no less dangerous act of rebellion and resistance, was becoming an actual "thing". In response our own local police departments were ratcheting up their drug investigations and harassment. "Busts" were spiking upward and people were looking at heavy jail time for possession of a mere joint let alone an ounce or two. The specter of the "narcs" was on everybody's radar and the act of actually enjoying being high was always tempered with rational paranoia.

It was against this backdrop of circumstances that a remarkable series of events unfolded. The tale is told variously by many who claim to be in the know, but there are those who actually had a front row seat, and from what I've heard, the story goes something like this — and I'll tell it as faithfully as I can.

In 1969 or 1970 — it varies depending on who tells the story — a local Santa Cruz guy began to grow pot using Cannabis sativa seeds from "landrace" varieties (adapted in their regions of origin). Some versions of the story point to a local surfer named G, who "backcrossed his 'punto rojo' (Columbian red)" while others start the begats from the second of the, by now, legendary "Haze Brothers", R.L., who might have crossbred a red or Oaxacan with a landrace from southern India and then one from Thailand. The thing is, on the many web sites that carry some version of this history the details are always different. The actual exact sequence of events, and which specific varieties were involved is unclear and may never be known. But from these seeds an Ur cultivar emerged and set in motion the next several generations of a variety that henceforth became known famously, and the world over, as "Original Haze".

A profile on the Humboldt Seed Organization website states:

Throughout history, there've been many different strains (that) will be remembered 'till the end of time. But there was one strain in particular that simply appeared in the right place, at the right time, and so marked a before and an after in the history of the cannabis community.

Yes, we're talking about Haze. Of all the things that have raised this strain to the status of a legend, it is the mystery surrounding its creation that is to be blamed. The most popular theory is that it was the Haze Brothers and Sam "The Skunkman", the originator of the Skunk, who created it. Legend has it that back in the '70s, in the Californian region of Santa

Cruz, the cradle of cannabis culture of a country determined to end the use of cannabis, these curious guys decided to cross some cannabis lines from all over the world.

And from an account on "The Smoker's Club" website:

Haze is such an integral part of cannabis culture to this day. From the day's of Florida's Crypt Haze to Harlem's Uptown Haze to Amsterdam's masterpiece, Jack Herer, and, from any more recent haze hybrid you may have ever had the pleasure of puffing — they most likely all had their start from the reigning queen matriarch of the family… Original Haze.

There were several strains that emerged from the first generations of Haze, including Silver Haze and Green Haze, but the most famous was "Purple Haze". Like a great wine, with its complex scents and tastes, variously described as "incense", "sandalwood", "chocolate", and "citrus", and the color shading from reds and purples to pink and green stripes, this towering plant produced huge colas, that literally dripped, shimmered and sparkled with sticky resin. Moreover, the high associated with this strain is characterized as "uplifting", "powerful and energizing" as well as "psychedelic" and "long lasting".

Part of the legend of Haze revolves around how the strains that followed in the succeeding decades were created and marketed. Countless varieties now are available around the world and some are indica hybrids of the original all-sativa forms. The distribution and varietal palette seems to be less disputed but nevertheless not without controversy. But I'll leave that up to you readers to explore and decide for yourselves.

Some say the first crosses were grown in back of a ramshackle cottage in Live Oak, and some advocate for other spots around the hills of Santa Cruz. But the first hybrids may actually have been created in a couple of adjoining backyards on a quiet street in a sleepy neighborhood on the west side of the Cruz, not far from Professor Abraham's abode. Within a few years the grand experiment shifted locations to a more rural setting near the edge of town, a stones throw into the Banana Belt, and as word got around and local growers began to create their own varieties and maneuver and negotiate for seeds, the whole enterprise shifted into a larger scale/marketing phase. Whereas an ounce of reg would cost you twenty-five bucks in the "old days", an ounce of Haze, if you could get it, was two to four hundred. The Haze Brothers were trying out marketing gimmicks like selling large colas in separately crafted wooden cigar-type boxes, with a small copy of the now famous Purple Haze poster glued on the inside of the lid. Lawyers and doctors and mortgage brokers were snapping them up like candy. It had the feel of a mini "tulip bulb mania", a-la seventeenth century Holland.

Eventually, seeds made their way around the globe, especially to Amsterdam, where another legendary breeder/grower/marketing maven took things to a trans-national level and the rest is history. And right here I'll end this tale, but with one more critically important point about Hip Santa Cruz' impact on the world stage:

It has been said that the victors write history. I like to say that history is mainly the past with an army and a navy. But that would be showing a lack of respect. One of the reasons the history of Haze is as unstable as the "phenos" of the original cultivars, full of disputes and claims as to who was the real Mr. Numero Uno, is due to the fact that it wasn't necessarily a he. Let me explain. When the first strains of Haze were being created over in that sleepy little neighborhood previously mentioned, it was actually a couple of women who were experimenting with hybridization, soil mixes, organic fertilizing, astrological alignments, and indoor versus outdoor growing. One of the Haze brothers was involved, but it must be noted that, as far as my front row source can remember, the Haze Bro was learning the ropes and it was those two gals who had the mega-green thumbs. Between them they created the breeding/growing environment that led to the first fine strains, and what followed over the next couple of years took place among a small group of people who were also experimenting, swapping seeds and knowledge. You see, it actually does take a village.

P.S. *As a center of liberal and progressive activism, Santa Cruz became one of the first cities to approve marijuana for medicinal uses. In 1992, residents overwhelmingly approved Measure A, which allowed for the medicinal uses of marijuana. Santa Cruz was home to the second above-ground medical marijuana club in the world when the Santa Cruz Cannabis Buyers Club opened its doors in April 1995. Santa Cruz also became one of the first cities in California to test the state's medical marijuana laws in court after the arrest of Valerie Corral and Mike Corral, founders of the Wo/Men's Alliance for Medical Marijuana, by the DEA. The case was ruled in favor of the growers. In 2005, the Santa Cruz City Council established a city government office to assist residents with obtaining medical marijuana. On November 7, 2006, the voters of Santa Cruz passed Measure K by a vote of 64-36 percent. [Wikipedia: Santa Cruz, California]*

Put that in your pipe and smoke it!

Chapter 10: Misha B. Adams
I Picked It Out of a Book

When I decided to come to California in 1970, I was a college dropout working as a secretary in Washington, D.C. It was a harsh, gloomy winter in the District of Columbia, and my fiancée was serving in the army in Vietnam. I lived in a funky apartment in the hippie district of North West Washington, two blocks from Dupont Circle. My friends were a gaggle of hip-folk, some of whom I'd lived with two years previously in an urban commune when I first arrived in D.C. with my then husband, also a soldier. Between that early marriage and my current affianced relationship, I saved up enough money to go back to El Paso, Texas for another year of college. That was where I met this tall, erudite Yankee-boy, fell in love, and trekked back to D.C. with my new boyfriend, whom the Army had ordered to report there for M.I. specialty school before being deployed overseas.

It was right after Christmas. Soggy snow plopped against my window on the third floor. I shivered in my R Street apartment, trying to keep my two Siamese cats from fighting. I was reading a photo essay a friend had given me for Christmas — The California Feeling, by Peter Beagle. It was an enthralling read. I noticed that when the book was published, the author happened to be living in the Northern California town of Santa Cruz. I thought it looked like my kind of place.

Just then the plaster in the ceiling of my bathroom gave way and landed in the tub with a horrendous crunch! Given the lackadaisical work ethic of our building super, I knew I was in for weeks of surviving on sponge-baths. I really was not happy to become an indoor camper. I looked at the book, lying open to a photo of Santa Cruz … looked at the bathtub full of plaster … and decided it was time to move. Next day I turned in my notice at work and started paring down my belongings to what would fit in a car. I'd never been to Santa Cruz, though I'd visited Carmel once on a quick car trip from Las Vegas. I didn't know a single person who lived in California, but I had a deep and passionate longing to get myself there as soon as possible, by any means necessary.

In the '60s and '70s there were these things called *drive-away cars*. People who wanted to save money on shipping their automobiles to a new location could pay a modest fee to an agency and other people, who wanted to save money on travel, could contract with that business to drive the car from point A to point B, paying only for the gas and oil. It was a deal. I'd already done it twice: once to get from Texas to D.C. with my first husband, and then again, after a divorce and squeezing in another year of college in Texas, to return to Washington with my new guy. I signed up for a drive-away car from D.C. to El Paso.

Well, that turned out to be an adventure. I wanted to save every possible nickel and dime to invest in my new life in California, so I loaded some stuff, mostly books, my two cats and my guitar into the drive-away and hit the road. I saved cash on the way by sleeping in the common rooms of college dorms.

Unfortunately, one morning when I came out to feed the quarreling cats, I found an ugly dent in the headlight extension panel of my late-model drive-away auto. Yikes! I was motoring up the road outside Nashville in a state of panic when I saw, off to the side of the freeway, an auto dealership specializing in that very brand of car. I waited in the parking lot for them to open, and then asked the boss what it would take to fix the dent. The shop manager, a nice old guy with pictures of his grandkids on his cluttered desk, took pity on me when I told him my sad story. It turned out they had the part I needed in stock, as well as the matching paint. What they didn't have was a receptionist and their phones were going berserk. So, I jumped in and started fielding calls, sorting their mail, and squaring away teetering piles of files. I worked for the couple of hours it took them to spray paint and replace the headlight panel, we called it even, and my cats and I got back on the freeway headed for Texas.

The rest of the trip was uneventful and I made it to El Paso in a couple of days. My mother picked me up there after I surrendered the drive-away car. She drove the cats and me, and what was left of my belongings 180 miles south to our hometown of Alpine where she and my grandmother lived. I off-loaded the cats, (my mom already had seventeen cats, two more wouldn't make much difference,) rested up for a few weeks, and then packed a duffle bag for the last leg of my trip.

My mom and grandma drove me back to the El Paso airport where I bought a one-way ticket and got on a plane for San Francisco. My plan was to fly there and take a Greyhound down to Santa Cruz. I was carrying a compact sleeping bag and had my clothes and a few books in the duffle, along with a butcher knife, a whetstone, and a flint gizmo that could be used to start a fire. I'm still not sure why I thought I needed those, but they seemed important at the time.

I got off the plane at SFO and made my way downtown to the bus station, where I chucked my guitar in a locker and bought a ticket for Santa Cruz. It was pouring rain when we rolled into the bus station. Looking around at the clean streets and well-maintained buildings, and expecting the bus terminal to be located in a slum, as most of the other ones I'd seen had been, I remember thinking to myself, "Holy shit! If this is what passes for slums in this town, I'm doomed."

Two other bedraggled passengers and I were huddling in the Greyhound foyer staring out at the rain when a group of merry-looking pranksters scooped us up and invited us home to crash on their floor. They turned out to be UCSC students who were having a party that night.

We three drowned rats crept into our sleeping bags in a quiet corner that wouldn't stay quiet for long. I slept while the rising turbulence of the student party gave me surrealistic dreams. By morning I had learned some of the mythology of hip Santa Cruz: tales of political throw-downs, explosions of innovative music, sex, art and theater, and tales of a magical venue called The Catalyst.

These are some of the adventures I had during my first two weeks in town:

Stayed a week with a couple of local girls who taught me how to fish for, cook, and eat crabs from the wharf.

Got a job at a surplus store because the clerk was out on medical leave.

While on lunch break at the hippie deli next door, I overheard that "The Blaine House Studs" needed a housemate. More about them later.

Due to seeing and smelling so much of it around, I got the mistaken impression that marijuana was legal. Compared to both D.C. and Texas, it might as well have been.

I was laid off from the clerk job when the original clerk came back, but immediately got another job as an all-purpose gopher in a dress shop on the Mall. The owner let me ride up to San Francisco to help her on a buying trip to the garment district, and I was able to retrieve my guitar from the bus station locker.

I located those mysterious "Blaine House Studs" in a big old Victorian house behind the jail and Chuck, the commune's Old Sea-Dad, rented me the front room for so little money that I was able to afford it with my meagre clerking pay.

Of the six individuals living at Blaine Street, I was the only woman. This demographic mix was to be repeated often during my four-plus decades of living in Santa Cruz. My late psychologist mom might have sarcastically characterized it as the "Snow White Syndrome."

When the dress shop gig showed signs of petering out, I looked for other employment. The Blaine Street Commune where I was living — as you will probably read in other essays in this collection — had been the home of the first underground newspaper in Santa Cruz: *The Free Spaghetti Dinner*. Before I moved in, the paper changed hands and was now being run by an artists' collective upstairs in a building on Pacific Garden Mall. My Blaine St. brothers told me they heard the paper needed a typist. I immediately hoofed it downtown and tromped up the stairs to knock on the door of the newspaper, now known as *Sundaz!*

The door creaked open and thick clouds of cannabis smoke billowed out, filtering through the waist-length hair of local artist Kentus Americanus, one of the publishers. I flashed him my best Texas smile and brightly announced, "Hi! I'm your new typist!"

Kent took a long pull on a fat joint, and, while holding in that righteous hit, wheezed, "You're hired." I started right away. Every week I typed the whole paper on rolls of adding machine paper, which was both cheap, as office supplies went, and made for easy column layout. I earned the cash to pay my rent and buy food, and had enough left over to buy stamps so I could mail letters to my beloved, who by then was stationed at an American military base near the An Khê Pass between Qui Nhơn and Pleiku in the Central Highlands of Vietnam.

For a young woman (in those days I still would have referred to myself as a 'chick') recently arrived from Washington, D.C., hip communal life in Santa Cruz required some cultural adjustment. I had only ever been a five o'clock hippie when the whistle blew. I always had a legal, paying job, a place to live, and most of the necessities of what then constituted lower-middle-class existence.

The first thing I did was to stop straightening my hair. It soon reverted to the kinky wilderness that was its natural state. It had been the bane of my existence throughout the '60s when stick-straight-haired Yardley Girls were our fashion icons. When my poor fiancée got off the bus in Santa Cruz a year later and saw my hair looking like an unruly thatched roof, I could see the dismay in his eyes!

One day I was busily scrubbing away in the Blaine House bathtub when Tall Paul, one of the famous Barn Bros. Furniture Building dudes, came into the bathroom to take a whizz. He was easily tall enough to see over the shower curtain where I was cowering, mortified, in the back of the tub. He dispensed a kernel of wisdom that was to stand me in good stead during the whole assimilation process to come: "Don't worry, you'll mellow out!" He was right. I eventually did.

I loved every minute of living in Blaine House and some of my housemates have remained up close in my life ever since. Chief among them is Rick Gladstone, who became my political mentor and guru and also a role model for writing, playing and performing original music. Over the past decades, we have been and continue to be sworn siblings. He was at my wedding and I attended his. We have seen one another's babies come into the world, grow up, go off to college and begin to weave their own webs of kinship. We have helped our parents live out their final years here and grieved together when their lives ended. Rick was my very first friend in this town and I will treasure his friendship forever.

My memories of living at Blaine House and working at *Sundaz!* in 1971 are stuffed with images of intense afternoons spent drinking strong coffee in the Catalyst while Tom Scribner educated us about the early years of the Wobbly movement; rock concerts featuring up-and-coming local bands like Snail, and Sons of Champlin, the Doobie Brothers, and Jango; moonlight incursions onto the UCSC campus to peer like feral animals at those fortunate sons and daughters, living their privileged lives with their superb recreational drugs and highfalutin phraseology; and plenty of real-life action and adventure like the time a bunch of us were running a lemonade stand at a music festival, at Pinto Lake when a brawl broke out between bikers and locals. Those were the days, my friends!

    I was still working for *Sundaz!* in 1971 when my intended spouse returned from overseas to land in Santa Cruz, a town he'd never seen except in the photos I had mailed him. We pooled our resources — what remained of his military pay, and my earnings at the newspaper, and moved into a little bungalow across from what was then Laurel Elementary School and is now the Louden Nelson Community Center.

    In the fall of that year we got married. We had a proper hippie wedding in the back yard at Blaine House. Our friend Chuck, the Blaine Street head of household, became a mail-order Universal Life Church Minister so that he could perform our ceremony. My husband wore a shirt I embroidered for him and I wore a wreath of flowers on my head. I went up to the UCSC garden early that morning to pick the flowers. As I was driving up the hill a magnificent owl floated down right in the glare of my headlights, gave me a haughty stare, and took off again like an apparition from a sword and sorcery novel. I took it as a favorable omen.

    Three days later we very consciously and intentionally brought about the conception of our daughter, whom we would name Deirdre Danielle Scripture-Adams. A few months into my pregnancy I realized I was too exhausted to continue working, so I quit. What a weird feeling that was, being financially dependent on another person! I hadn't been in that situation since I was a high school kid living in a dysfunctional single-parent family in West Texas. By mid-year I couldn't stand the inactivity any longer, so I enrolled in Cabrillo Community College. I caught a city bus out to the school from town, took theater classes, and got biology credit for growing an organic garden on a plot the school provided for that purpose.

At the beginning of Spring Semester, I signed up for a course that was to change my life: Introduction to Physical Anthropology, taught by James J. Funaro. I had little or no interest in the subject of anthropology, but I had a vague notion that I might someday like to transfer into the University of California, Santa Cruz, and I needed another social science credit to be eligible for that.

From the very first day, when, *great with child*, I heaved myself, panting and wheezing up the hill from the bus stop to Funaro's class, I was totally mesmerized by the subject being taught. Funaro was, and is, a phenomenal teacher. He was also notorious among politically aware female students for being an unapologetic sexist. If I'd stopped to think about that at the time, I'd probably have been put off by Jim's uber-macho reputation. As it was, I had fallen so stark-raving in love with the subject of anthropology that I was gazing at my text books with little red valentines popping out of my eyes like a character from a Warner Bros. cartoon.

Here's another reason why I didn't give a rip what the other women students thought of Funaro: we read, and he lectured about field research being done on colonies of baboons in Africa, and about how these studies were contributing to emerging theories of early human biological and social evolution. One day after class I went to his desk and said to Funaro, "Hey Jim… all this stuff they're writing about in here seems to be mostly about *male* baboons. How come there's nothing about what's going on with the *females*?

Now that would have been the perfect time for my professor to launch into a screed about the evolutionary importance of dominance hierarchies and *Alpha Males,* and the like…

But he didn't. Instead, Jim told me that up until recently, most of the existing primate field research had been conducted by men, and that they probably tended to pay more attention to the kinds of behaviors that they, themselves were most interested in. He then told me if I was bothered by how little material there was on female primates, I should get my degrees and go out and do research about them myself! Bless him!

So, I did. Get my degrees in anthropology, that is — not become a primate researcher — but I have never forgotten the graceful way Professor Funaro handled my question.

We expected our daughter to be born late in the summer of 1972 and Danny and I were convinced we wanted to have Lamaze natural childbirth. We took classes at the Santa Cruz Midwives' Collective and engaged Kitty Lakos, also a Registered Nurse, to be our midwife. I also signed up with Dr. Ralph Kemp, a local obstetrician who favored the Lamaze technique, but was against home birth, which he believed to be foolhardy and dangerous for both mother and child.

As my due date got closer, my husband was adamant that he did not want the baby to be born at home. I would have been happy with a home birth, and, although we argued about it, I finally acquiesced. But I told both my husband and the doctor that I would not consent to a hospital delivery unless my midwife could join us in the delivery room. The doctor reluctantly agreed, and Kitty, who was just as turned off by hospital births as Dr. Kemp was by home deliveries, agreed to come with us to Community Hospital and assist with my labor and delivery.

My mother and my eighty-eight-year-old grandmother drove here from Texas to be part of the event. I started having contractions early in the morning on the 30th of July 1972. My husband, after working the night shift cleaning the *Santa Cruz Sentinel* newspaper building, was sleeping like a hibernating bear. I labored peacefully by myself for four hours, but eventually I had to wake him up and call Kitty and my mom. He groggily asked if I'd put the coffee on. I told him to go to hell. He jumped up, realized it was really happening, and sprang into action like the crisis-trained Vietnam vet that he was. Kitty and my mother showed up shortly after that.

My mother, who had suffered through an appallingly difficult childbirth with me, arrived looking dead-pale and emitting high voltage anxiety. She was so nervous that I began to worry more about her than my own contractions. That was when Kitty kindly but firmly 86'ed her from the house, telling her to meet us at the hospital. Once my mom left, I relaxed and found the contractions didn't hurt as much as I'd thought. When they were three minutes apart we drove to the hospital and checked into the labor room.

Kitty took over from the O.B. nurses and cared for me with consummate skill as my contractions got stronger. She showed my husband how to massage my back and make me as comfortable as possible. When I began to transition into third-stage labor, Dr. Kemp arrived and asked me if it would be OK for his wife and two kids to join my mother and grandma in the waiting room, where they could watch the delivery on closed-circuit TV. I had no objections. Soon after that my dear friend Erainya Nierro, whom we'd chosen to be the baby's godmother, also joined the waiting room cheering section.

The whole event unfolded a lot faster than anybody had predicted. These next items may not mean much to those of you who have never attended a childbirth, but I had no enema; no prep; no anesthetic of any kind; no stirrups on the delivery table; and no episiotomy. I gave birth to our healthy eight-pound daughter while sitting up and holding on to my knees with Kitty and my husband supporting my back. In fact, after the baby was born, I had about six or seven hours' worth of excess adrenalin coursing through my body. I'd never been so high in my life! Dr. Kemp joked that the birth had been so easy, I might just want to get up and walk out! To his and everybody else's shock, that's exactly what I did. I climbed off the table, took my swaddled baby in my arms, and walked out of the room and down the hall to the nursing station where I gave a short lecture on the benefits of Lamaze natural childbirth. My grandmother started laughing and my mom fainted.

This is a good place to point out that we were big-mouthed, opinionated, white, college educated, and ostensibly middle-class people, despite our hippie demeanor and due to our privilege and audacity, we got away with things that, even in that time and place, were patently outrageous. If I'd tried a stunt like that today I'd probably get tackled to the floor by hospital security guards and charged with child endangerment! Plus, since we were counter-culture to the core, the very first sound my daughter heard was my voice singing a song I'd written for her during the nine months that we shared a common corporeal reality.

In the fall of 1973, a year after our lovely baby was born, I enrolled at UCSC as a junior transfer student. Back then, we were known as *re-entry* or *non-traditional students*. Privately,

I referred to myself as a drop-back-in, since I had jumped in and out of college several times in the prior decade, depending on what else was happening in my life. Truth be told, I still wasn't completely sure I even **was** *college material.*

When I started taking classes on "The Hill," as we townspeople called it, I was intimidated all to hell by the younger, more affluent, probably smarter, and definitely more confident college students who shared my classrooms. By then my husband and I had moved into married student housing on the west side of the campus and we were very busy parenting our little girl while working and going to school. My husband was commuting to San Jose State, where he was enrolled in a graduate program in Linguistics. He was still working nights as a janitor at the *Santa Cruz Sentinel* newspaper.

The first time I showed up to see my assigned academic advisor, I grumpily expected him to be some kind of elitist Oxford Don. Instead, I was delighted to find that the University computer, in its infinite wisdom, had assigned me a counselor from Germany who was only few years older than I. He, himself, had been a re-entry student. A man with a young family, he had returned to college after serving in the military. He was the perfect person to advise me about managing my time, mustering the courage to speak up in class, and he even encouraged me to make friends with younger undergraduates, some of whom remain close friends of mine today.

I majored in Community Studies. Politics and the struggles for human rights interested me more and more. Anthropology was still important to me but the other curriculum fit better with the coursework I had already completed in college in Texas. I knew that if I wanted to earn a Bachelor's degree on such a severely limited budget, I had to make every credit count.

The Community Studies academic major required us to complete a six-month full-time field study. I was lucky to get a paying job with the Santa Cruz County Office on Aging, developing a grant and applying to the Federal Older Americans Act for funding to establish community resource information and referral centers for senior citizens in our county. Little did I suspect that I would live here long enough to avail myself of some of those very services!

My professor and field study advisor at UCSC was the notable anti-war and social justice political activist Jim Mellon, who had been one of the framers of the Port Huron Statement — the principal manifesto of SDS. The first time I went into Jim's office to report on my recent field study activities, I mumbled on and on about "The Elderly, "The Unemployed," and "The Lower Income…" After several tortured minutes, Jim interrupted me and asked, "Is it *them*, or do you really talk like that?" I burst into tears. I had an epiphany: I realized that, as a Community Studies scholar, my boundaries were too permeable and I was too unskilled at critical thinking to be allowed to go out into the world and cause stuff like this to happen that could actually affect vulnerable people's lives. The truth was that I could not trust myself not to suck up and perpetrate casual injustices under the rubric of "helping those less fortunate than myself."

That was what caused me to, as they say in the military, *re-up* in Anthropology after completing my Community Studies degree. Rather than graduate in spring of 1974, I filed for a double academic major in Community Studies *and* Anthropology and stayed in college an additional year. My rationale was that, since the field of anthropology seemed to have fewer easy answers to global problems and not as many fixed and immutable categories as some of its fellow social sciences, this would be an academic discipline that might do a better job of keeping me honest. That's how I came to return to the object of my intellectual lust at Cabrillo. I was ecstatic to find that absence had only made my heart grow fonder.

I completed the Anthro. major and graduated with a B.A. in Community Studies and Anthropology at the end of the 1974/75 academic year. By then, I had developed a strong interest in cultural anthropology, communication, and women's studies. During my time as an undergraduate I met and was impressed with several students in UCSC's interdisciplinary graduate program, the History of Consciousness. My husband, who was still pursuing his studies at San Jose State, was a graduate of Goddard College in Vermont — one of a handful of small, innovative liberal arts colleges that encouraged their students to combine academic disciplines. He had heard of Hist. Con., as we called it, and that was one reason why he was willing to relocate with me to Santa Cruz after his discharge from the military.

Both my husband and I applied to the program and, to my astonishment, I was accepted, first as an alternate, and then, when the first-choice candidate, who also happened to be a dear friend of mine, was unethically persuaded by her faculty advisor to opt for a different institution, I had the opportunity to enroll as a graduate student in Hist. Con. I thought I must be dreaming. Upstart hippie chick from the Texas outback goes to graduate school! What a concept!

I began the History of Consciousness program in 1975 and finished with a PhD and parenthetical degree notation in Anthropology in 1980. This meant, essentially, that, should an academic institution wish to hire me without being sure they believed there even *was* such a thing as an '*interdisciplinary graduate program*', they could close their eyes, hold their nose, and take it on faith that I had at least completed the requirements for a doctorate in cultural ethnography.

As a famously malapropos friend of mine would say, *for all intensive purposes*, I was an anthropologist, albeit of a somewhat quirky variety.

While I was in graduate school, one of my research topics was Deaf/hearing communication contexts. I took lessons in and became fairly fluent in American Sign Language. The professors on my doctoral committee were skeptical when I asked to be allowed to use ASL as one of the two non-English languages required in order to graduate. They argued over this until Professor May Diaz commented that Cambridge University had allowed world-famous paleontologist Louis Leakey to take his language exam in Swahili. That settled it. My sponsor in the Santa Cruz Deaf community, Mr. Rex Ross, a local printer, came up to the University and conducted my language examination in ASL in the presence of my committee. I passed.

In addition to Professor Diaz, I studied with several notable and brilliant anthropologists including Dr. Carolyn Martin-Shaw, Dr. Adrienne Zihlman, Dr. Nancy Tanner, and Dr. David Schneider, who was on loan to us from the University of Chicago. I was privileged to have the eminent Language and Gender theorist, Dr. Barrie Thorne, a visiting professor from UC Berkeley as my ex-officio committee member. Through an improbable and semi-mystical quirk of time and space, I placed a fan phone call that resulted in a long-distance correspondence with the world-renowned Science Fiction author, Samuel R. Delany, who later became a professor of Comparative Literature at U. Mass. Amherst and Temple University. Had it not been for Mr. Delany's kind and generous tutoring, I could never have finished my dissertation. But at UCSC, my chief mentor was a true interdisciplinary scholar, Dr. Gregory Bateson. Studying with him was the greatest intellectual experience of my life.

While I was an undergraduate and graduate student at UCSC in the last half of the decade of the 1980s, I also busked folk music on the streets of Santa Cruz and at college nights with a fellow anthropology student, Roy David S. Kaplan. Roy and I wrote and sang our own original songs, many of which encapsulated our experiences and enthusiasms in academia. Roy used to call me "the Queen of Doggerel" on account of my tendency to write funny songs about serious and sometimes disturbing topics, including my college coursework. Describing what I really learned in graduate school would take up far more space than could be allotted to me here. Instead, I'd like to offer one of the songs I wrote about that experience. What did Hist. Con. mean to me? This is as close as I can come to summing it up:

TALKIN' HIST CON BLUES
Well I dropped back in just to get my degree
Thought I might go for the PhD
History 'a Consciousness
History 'a **what**?
History 'a whatever-the-hell-they-got

We had a lot of sub-groups back in them days
We had groups for straights and groups for gays
Groups about Kant and groups about Hegel
Groups for folks who'd never seen a bagel
Cultural diversity … in the University

We had a lot of clout
We had Student Power
We had revolution 'bout every other hour
A stake in the government and what was required
We knew who was hired and sometimes who was fired

'Till the folks on top thought we looked a little strong
Said "Put them students back where they belong…
Hittin' the books, 'stead 'a runnin' the Program!"

No more hassle, no more fuss
No more politic'n people like us
From now on it'll be done right
They're bringin' in a fella called Hayden White

(**Was** Hayden white?
You betcha!)

Now Hayden had a vision that we could project
And he had a reputation they had to respect
I felt like a street kid, raised to glory
And put into the chorus of *West Side Story*

Nowadays, when they ask, 'Hist Con… what do you hiss?'
We say: "Vulgar Marxism!"
"Naïve Empiricism!"
And "*conscious* sexism!"

We got the *context,* the *pretext,* the *topos,* the *trope*
Irony, synecdoche, and world-class dope
We do Derridian deconstruction and it don't leave a *Trace*
We got *Fruitful Bodies,* so get off our case!
We had Bateson and Natanson, Marcuse and Brown
But now we got the baddest, meanest game in town!
Eat your hearts out, Social Thought!
Back off, Brandeis! **Here come the Sphinx!**

Here I am, forty-eight years after picking Santa Cruz out of a book and straggling into town with a guitar and a duffel bag. I can truly say that I wouldn't have chosen to live anywhere else, or any other way.

Chapter 11: Frank Foreman
Caffe Hip History

Judy & Frank Foreman moved to Santa Cruz because parking anywhere near their North Beach railroad flat had become impossible, and housing in the Bay Area was unaffordable for a public school teacher to rent, or buy. After leaving our daughter with friends vacationing in Santa Cruz, I spent the afternoon with the son of my grad school advisor getting stoned in the redwoods at UCSC. We decided Santa Cruz was a pleasant, affordable place and we started house hunting in the summer of 1972.

In the Beginning

The Caffe Pergolesi was Frank and Judy's art project that posed as a business. Neither of us had experience in the restaurant world. I lasted one night as a dishwasher in a fancy restaurant in Tiburon in 1958, leaving in disgust. We had no clue how difficult it would become, so much so that we were ready to give up during the first year. We somehow managed to keep the Caffe running successfully for three years, even making a modest profit in the first month. Shop keepers we were not. Was this art as a business, or business as art?

Late in 1972 we moved into our newly purchased duplex in Santa Cruz near UCSC. I commuted Highway One to my job teaching half time in San Francisco. Judy looked for work, but only found temporary jobs. Missing the Caffe Trieste in North Beach, we considered starting a coffee house which Judy would manage and make jewelry during the slow times. We built a drawer for her jewelry equipment. Never did she make jewelry at the Caffe. We became friends with Ron and Sharon Lau, the owners of Bookshop Santa Cruz. We suggested our cafe idea as a natural fit with the bookshop.

In summer of 1973 we began construction of the cafe in the brick shed behind the bookshop. We, with a lot of help from our friends, remodeled the inside of the "watermelon" room, installed an oak floor, plumbed and electrified the place, created two entrances from the newly constructed deck, built a counter and tables, purchased bent-wood chairs and a few pews. Gianni Giotta of the Caffe Trieste sold us, on time, the La Cimbali three group espresso machine, grinder and other necessary equipment. We used their coffee bean supplier: Capricorn Coffee in the City. After nine months of long days sand blasting the outside walls of the entire bookshop, we transformed a brick storage room into a coffee house.

The city planning department was not obstructionist and the permit fees were reasonable, unlike current practices. We were required to install reinforcing steel rods to prevent the brick walls from collapsing during an earthquake. The walls cracked, but did not fail during the 1989 Loma Prieta quake.

Judy, Lynn and I spent two days in training at the Trieste with Gianfranco, Rita and Yolanda. Our teachers were pros and we learned lots quickly. Of course, we had spent years observing them at work which helped set our high standards.

Why Pergolesi? Judy was delighted to learn about Giovanni B. Pergolesi while attending UC Santa Barbara. She related to me that Pergolesi was born in 1710 at Jesi, Italy and died of dissipation in 1736. We liked his music and admired that he lived his short life to the fullest. Death by excessive indulgence in wine, women and song deserved to be honored. Therefore, we named our caffe after him. Most likely he died of TB, which I too contracted upon our return from six months of hitchhiking and hosteling in Europa.

Judy learned to do the books and make sure the espresso jerks were paid on time and that all taxes and related reporting was done. As the Boss, Judy fired three and rehired one worker. Slothfulness was the usual reason. I took care of gathering supplies, maintenance, entertainment and things Judy did not want to do. We both worked the counter many hours each week, and all too often covered for a worker who failed to show up for work.

Our caffe was a highly personal statement of our aesthetic. We had experienced cafes in Europa and were especially fond of those in Italy. We put our stamp on the Caffe Pergolesi as the kind of place we would like for a hang out. Our goal was to create a caffe with Japanese austerity, the elegance of cafes in Vienna, combined with the camaraderie of an Italian caffe, while capturing the easy going attitudes of North Beach in the Sixties. The Caffe Trieste in North Beach clearly represented the combined ideas of the Giotta family we knew and admired. The Cafe Sperl in Vienna represented the visual and aural sophistication to which we aspired. The Caffe San Marco in Trieste set the standard for conviviality. Our efforts successfuly combined what we valued aesthetically, gastronomically and socially in a friendly, yet not a standard brand commercial coffee house.

Ah memory, she all too often eludes me. To remedy this lapse, I include the reminiscences of Caffe espresso jerks and customers randomly, and not so randomly, in this tract.

Why a caffe?

Carolyn Burke was wondering why she left Paris for this backward small town. She had a young child and by accident discovered the caffe. She says it saved her life. Used to cafe life in Paris, she finally had a place in which to write as her daughter Poppy grew up in an atmosphere conducive for writing her first biography about the poet Mina Loy. She mentioned the topic of her writing to me and was surprised I knew about Mina Loy and had even read her *Lunar Baedecker*.

We became fast friends, and still are, three more biographies later. Carolyn also wrote limericks as a diversion.

In Praise of the Pergolesi

Where else could one drink such caffe
As will set you right up for the day,
Eat cream cheese and bagel
While pondering Hegel
And never be rushed on your way?

Poetic Bliss at the Pergolesi

While consuming a fresh baked croissant
In my favorite coffeehouse haunt,
I curled up with the Times
And composed a few rhymes —
What else could a poor poet want?

Doug Montalbano excerpts from a college essay:
In a fit of malaise, I had quit my job of five years; soon after that my lover and I broke up.
Fortunately, during that February a coffeehouse opened for business behind the bookshop. I had read about these places — European cities were full of them: cafes where you could sit for an hour or two over a cup of coffee, read various newspapers (supplied by the management), listen to Baroque or modern classical music, talk to people, or, on pleasant days, drowse in the sun. Here in our out-of-the-way corner of California (by way of San Francisco's North Beach) was such a caffe. The coffee and ambience were excellent, created by proprietors who seemed friendly but definitely not the usual small business types. They refused to play rock music or allow smoking; they behaved

casually instead of obsequiously; they appeared to have senses of humor. Of this couple Frank seemed to be the prankster. He would sometimes challenge the customer to "roll the die" for his coffee; if the customer's number came up he would get the drink free, if not he would pay double. Such was his manner that a surprisingly large number of people would agree to this and cheerfully pay up if they lost.

His way of disposing of leftover cream puffs remains unique. If they were more than a day old, he'd announce that they would be given away, no charge, to anyone who would receive one squashed gently in the face (towel provided). Again, to my astonishment, people took up his offer. Clearly, this couple knew something about human nature. I became a habitue of the Caffe."

Frank

Doug was a bit off. We would never sell day old cream puffs or eclairs. However, late at night I would make the offer of one free, so the thing would not be day old the next day, at the roll of the die. If odd it would be gently smashed in my face, even in the customer's. Of course, I varied the choices each night.

What was the Caffe really like?

How to explain about what it was like, you had to have been there. I am trying to give something of the flavor we worked hard to maintain. One of our goals was making it a meeting place for all kinds of people: students, professors, artists, poets, politicos, musicians, the retired, street people, lawyers, a good cross section of the community. Most definitely we kept it from becoming a student ghetto. We attracted customers of all ages and backgrounds, I guess it is called diversity these days.

Janet Ing reports on the flypaper incident:

I was working the night the flypaper came off the fan — the other duty officer was Doug, who went into something of a panic as a very sweet child approached the counter, shaking and speechless and pointing to his head, which was covered with gooey paper and dead flies. But for the life of me I can't remember what we did. Hot water? Hot chocolate? Hot wet knife? (I still murmur 'hot wet knife' when cutting into sticky desserts.) What on earth did we say to his parents to talk them out of suing — it must have been good.

Money
The loan officer at County Bank laughed at us when we asked for a loan to start the caffe. He was incredulous that providing coffee and pastries would make for a successful business. Starbucks first opened a few years earlier, but was not yet the monster it is now. So, we asked friends Don & Lynn for a $2,000 loan, which we paid back in six months. We made money the first month, enough to pay staff a little above the minimum hourly wage. We paid our bills on time, later realizing that was not a common business practice. We, early on, realized that we would not make any money until we sold the place. Amazingly, we sold our art project caffe for more than we earned on sales of our more traditional art during our life time. Had we been able to keep the business a few more years, we would have easily doubled the sale price. But, had we not sold, the chances are we would have divorced, or would have been institutionalized.

Halloween Parties 1974/5/6
We declared the Caffe closed for Jack Crick's birthdays. Our three Halloween parties fell on Jack's birthday, as did the other two or three days we closed for business. We never knew his actual birthday. Ecstatic dancing and bizarre wild

costumes ruled the nights. Andy Schiffrin had difficulty dancing in his filing cabinet costume. Frank came as the Dice Man super hero who frequently tossed foam dice extracted from his cod piece scrotum. In keeping with the times, many people were nearly nude in costumes which left very little to the imagination, in contrast with Judy and Teresa who wore elegant form-fitting silk dresses from the 1940s. I recall Hal Painter performing a sword dance with dangerously sharp weapons. Customers, staff and wandering strangers from the night danced to Clifton Chenier, rhythm & blues, rock and roll late into the night.

Julie Marlow remembers:

The rabid Halloween Party where Scott Malpass dressed as a pink satin prick tangoing with ???" "I appeared wearing six braids attached to helium balloons.

Karen Smith

The best part was the first Halloween party. I danced with a file cabinet, Julie had her hair in balloons and there was an inscrutable mummy. I always remember the file cabinet as one of my true loves.

Christmas Party 1974

We had parties whenever we were moved to party, which was often. Santa tossed bags of marijuana on the crowded dance floor unnoticed by the dancers until the dance finished.

Caffe Olympics 1976

Judy thought it would be fun to have a parallel olympics with the one in Japan. The events she created, with her Dada sensibilities, sparked me and the staff to invent even more events. All events took place while the Caffe was open and serving unsuspecting customers.

PROGRAM
Lighting of the flame
4:00 PM - Invocation: The Rev. Alton F. Foreman ULC consort to Boss
4:01 PM - Hymn from la Cimbali
4:02 PM - Flight of the flies
4:03 PM - Noise in unison from assembled children
4:04 PM - Welcome by High Public Official
4:05 PM - Guest Celebrity speaking on morality and coffee
4:06 PM - Explication by the Boss (Judy)
4:07 PM - Welcome by random customer in native tongue
4:08 PM - Introduction of Officials:
   Judy & Frank, Doug, Victor, Nutzle, Bob Hall
4:09 PM - Blessing & group singing of Veni Creator Spiritus
4:10 PM - LET THE EVENTS COMMENCE —
5:45 PM - Clean up and awarding of prizes
6:00 PM - Closing prayer & passing the ashes of the flame
9:00 PM - Halloween Party - Wild dancing and drinking and …

Caffe Olympics Events

The perfect Caffe Latte
Dishwashing (points for speed and cleanliness)
Fastest and most thorough espresso machine cleaning
Cup and saucer stacking and balancing
Customer insulting
Elocution test
   (Suggested phrase: Do you want milk in your coffee?)
Gushiest treatment of customers (fawning, ass-kissing…)
Table cleaning and bussing
Cheesecake sculpture and/or cutting
Garbage stomping
What to do with day-old eclairs

Spontaneous events to be added
Added by staff: Nicest ass — <u>male</u> & female
14. Sexual innuendos over counter -
"What would <u>you</u> really like?"

Dan Landry was the winner of Customer Insulting with his arch final comment to the question "What is an espresso? First he suggested the young woman read the menu. At her third question he calmly stated, "You have asked three stupid questions, now order something or leave." Lisa gave him good competition.

Julie Marlow: "Cheesecake sculpting. Judy dropped the cheesecake upside down behind the counter & we scooped it up with spatulas to re-sculpture."

I recall, with certainty, Judy carrying a large slice of cheesecake into the middle of the caffe and intentionally dropping the thing with feigned shock. The task of the contestant was to reshape it so as to appear fresh. I forget who won this event. I do recall that Julie won the perfect caffe latte preparation, hands down.

I added an event: Creation of new drinks. Mine won by popular acclaim.

Caffe Vesuviano — set alight a rolled Amaretti Di Saronno cookie wrapper which slowly rises toward the ceiling as I make a cappuccino grande with orange syrup and crumble the cookie on the foamed milk as I catch the slowly descending ash in the center of the drink with a flourish. All done in less than one minute.

Penny University

The historian Page Smith contacted us after reading a piece we had written about coffee houses in some entertainment journal or another. He was taken by the notion of the "Penny

Universities" in 18th and 19th century London, where anyone could attend gatherings at coffee houses for the price of a cup of coffee. Each caffe featured luminaries in poetry, finance, science, politics and other topics who would hold forth and encourage lively discussion. Page asked if we might entertain the idea of a "Penny University" at our caffe? Naturally, we were delighted.

Valentine's Day 1974 was the Pre-Opening of the Caffe with the first meeting of the Penny University. Page, Paul Lee, Mary Holmes and others were our first customers. Jack Stauffacher, San Francisco typographer/philosopher paid for his espresso with a one thousand lira note, which we framed and proudly displayed. The Penny University became a legally recognized institution by the state, and is still functioning, after forty-four years, but at a different site. Initially, "classes" were held weekday afternoons with wide ranging topics from U.S. History issues, to philosophy, religion and current affairs. I recall Ralph Abraham teaching astrology. Paul and Page held weekly classes during the three years we had the Caffe. Lively discussions ensued, and I vaguely recall one about the invited PU attendees at a NASA conference on planetary exploration, or some such topic. Notables passing through Santa Cruz would speak at the PU. Some of the best known speakers were Carl Sagan, Huey Newton, Carlos Castaneda, and Daniel Berrigan, who joined us for our Sunday morning Gregorian chants. Poets and authors would come to the Caffe to continue discussions and readings begun earlier at Bookshop Santa Cruz.

Bob Hall

It was outside the Caffe that the Penny U. Celebrated its 10th Anniversary, with Page Smith, Paul Lee and other "Academics" in their robes conferred MA's and PH'D's on their "students" along with champagne and cake for the celebration.

At the tenth anniversary of the PU and Caffe Judy and I were awarded honorary PhDs in Humane and Enlightened Impulses for acting as god parents of the PU. I always include this honor in my CV.

Performances-Events-Happenings-Fooling around
The Caffe was a venue for impromptu musical performances, random unselfconscious happenings, events and lots of just fooling around.

Music Policy
Initially jazz and classical were the recommended musics for the Caffe. We stored most of our records and cassettes at the Caffe. The place immediately became too busy to change records while serving espresso so we opted for cassettes. Some of the workers played music unsuitable for our idea of the Caffe. Many of their selections Judy and I liked, but not for the Caffe Pergolesi. Finally, I wrote a three page memo, #49, delineating in detail the kind of music to be played at the Caffe. Music of Beethoven and before, with emphasis on Mozart, Bach, Albinoni, Handel, Byrd, Buxtehude, Purcell, Corelli and Gregorian chant. We deemed music by Lou Harrison and Harry Partch as pre-Beethoven. What was then called world music, especially Indonesian gamelan, Peking Opera, Japanese and Korean court music, was also encouraged. Had we been proper business types, we would have dictated it was good for business, and after all the place was not named the Caffe Pergolesi for no reason. Those in doubt were directed to look for the Caffe Pergolesi sign above the door. Some of the staff labeled me musical fascist, a pejorative I proudly wear.

Live music was varied and often impromptu. Ricardo Tunzi was a regular accompanied by Casey Keller, Paul Hostetter, Irene Herman, Janet Dows and many others. Jeffery played lute on many evenings. Irish music on concertina, penny whistle and spoons was heard frequently. Bagpipers Lisa Emmons and Brian Steeger were asked to play outside on the deck for obvious reasons. An older man, probably in his fifties, asked if he could play double bass for coffee. To our delight he played only Bach. We later discovered he was Ron Crotty, the original bassist with the Dave Brubeck quartet. Sterling Storm and Esmerelda entertained twice with a three minute opera about an Australian run over by a steamroller. Most musicians understood the kind of music we preferred for the Caffe, even Rambling Jack Elliot asked to play and graciously understood our refusal. Countless individuals played guitars, flutes, accordions and other instruments through the years. Scheduled events ranged from Paraguayan harp, to a French Horn Quartet, Sundanese Gamelan, the Santa Cruz Youth Orchestra played Pergolesi, Gebhardt Long's string trio played Mozart, Biber & more. Gebhardt would come to the Caffe with his violin to play a brief Biber piece for his daily coffee. Irene Herman often charmed us with solo cello and the St. Cecilia Society for the Preservation and Restoration of Gregorian Chant, Peking Opera and Other Endangered Things of Beauty held forth every Sunday morning with traditional Gregorian chant in Latin.

When there were too many people in the Caffe, or undesirables, we would play Peking Opera or Gregorian chant on the sound system. This practice is now universally used for various purposes, but generally to discourage undesirables from hanging out.

Why country music, or anything with a twang was not heard at the Caffe: I spent 1956 and 57 in the army in

Germany. Every morning the Armed Forces Network radio blasted country music throughout the barracks at 5:30. This aversion therapy worked well and has lasted sixty years.

Karen Smith:
When the place got full he placed a Japanese gaga tape into my palm silently. I obeyed and the premises emptied quickly. We sang Kyrie's instead of screaming. When the line got too long Frank wrote a sign, back in 3/4 hour. The customers just stood there in line.

Janet Ing Freeman
The caffe music policy forever altered my listening habits. I am completely incapable of enjoying anything written in the nineteenth century. There are many fine musical memories of the caffe: the terribly beautiful man who played lute at night; brass bands, bagpipes, and Irish groups; the chant of course; and most of all Gebhardt Long and his group playing [correct me if I am wrong, but I don't think I am] Mozart's quintet in E flat major K. 614.

Casey Keler on Ricardo Tunzi
Back then I earned my cappuccino grandes and cheese sticks by accompanying the mandolin stylings of Ricardo Tunzi on my guitar. I had a band. I was a regular folksinger on an awful TV show called Ruth Marie's Room. I played a solo act at the Shadowbrook and the Crow's Nest. I was on the radio advertising Union Grove Music. But all people knew about me was that I was the guy who accompanied Mr. Tunzi on the guitar.

Mr. Tunzi was a charming old Italian gentleman. He had come to America on a boat as a teenager and people on that boat remember him playing the mandolin on the way over. He built a trucking business during prohibition and made a modest living running sugar and molasses for bootleggers. And now he was retired in Felton with nothing to do but play the mandolin.

Mr. Tunzi was deaf. Well, not totally deaf, but pretty deaf. He had no idea. People would come over to him, point to his mandolin and say "What kind of instrument is that?" He would look at me as if I were his translator and I would yell in his ear, "WHAT KIND OF INSTRUMENT IS THAT, MR. TUNZI?" And he'd check his watch and answer, "Eleven-thirty."

Anyway, Mr. Tunzi and I had a regular evening gig at the Pergolesi which we played to support our caffeine habits and enjoy the atmosphere behind Book Shop Santa Cruz and so that I could meet the young women who came to hear Mr. Tunzi.

We knew Mr. Tunzi from the Caffe Trieste where he played mandolin for Saturday sing fests with Fabio, Giani, Gianfranco and others. Earlier in the day he would play with other Italian old men at a North Beach barber shop. We were surprised to find him living nearby, and delighted to have him play at our caffe.

Bob Hall

Being an out-of-doors kind of community the Santa Cruz Caffe life took advantage of the perfect weather. The veranda and patio in back provided the Cobblestone Courtyard space for some of the early performances by the Screaming Memees, The Flying Karamazov Brothers, and other talented groups such as Tom Noddy (of Bubble Magic fame) and Jan Lubey, and old Tom Scribner and his musical saw.

Tom Scribner, was the only person I ever spoke with who knew C.E.S. Wood. Tom collected money for the Wobblies from Wood at his Los Gatos estate, up the hill from the Cat Sculptures on Highway 17. C.E.S. Wood's books were important formative works for me. Tom played his musical saw for the opening party of the Caffe.

The Flying Karamazovs juggled inside the Caffe as well as outside. Pastries, cups, plates flew through the space with no breakage. Not having been on duty all of the time, I missed some performances.

St. Cecilia Society

The Saint Cecilia Society for the Preservation and Restoration of Gregorian chant, Peking Opera & Other Endangered Things of Beauty formed at the Caffe.

Frequently we played chant on the sound system at the Caffe because we loved the music we heard growing up in the Church. I invited a few friends to start a chant group. Jerry, Catholic chaplain and Herb Schmidt from UCSC, provided us with beginners chant books. We floundered for a couple of weeks until Dan Landry, a customer and later employee, who had been in a seminary and knew chant well, began teaching us. We founded the St. Cecilia Soc. on St. Cecilia's Feast Day, November 22, 1974. Forty-four years later we are still singing with many new members and five from the original group: Don Day, Craig Johnson, Don Cochrane, Dan Landry and me,

We surprised the composer Lou Harrison by chanting at his home on his sixtieth birthday. Lou immediately understood why I gave the group such a cumbersome name. In the 1960s two of the most entrenched imperial bureaucracies, the Chinese Communist Party had banned Peking Opera and the Roman Catholic Church, with Vatican II, by decreeing the mass be sung in vernacular, essentially eliminated Gregorian chant in Latin, save in a few monasteries. I felt tasked to remedy this travesty, in my quiet way, by founding the St. Cecilia Society at the Caffe Pergolesi. Lou was also aware that St. Cecilia Societies, generally Catholic lay people, promoted music, especially plainsong, throughout Europa and the Americas in the 19th and 20th centuries. I feel vindicated, but claim no influence, by the fact that Gregorian chant was appropriated by pop music, and traditional chant in Latin ranked high on pop music charts in the 1990s. Peking Opera has replaced revolutionary opera as a major tourist attraction and is commonly heard now in the Peoples Republic of China.

Lou dedicated his Mass for St. Cecilia's Day to The St. Cecilia Society. We performed his mass at various venues: Premiered by the St. Cecilia Society in our living room in 1985; at Mills College Special Collections Library; at St. Mark's church in San Francisco, and at the Santa Cruz New Music Works celebration of Lou's centenary in 2017. Some of our first performances were embarrassingly bad, but after about thirty years we have improved. Our group was the chorus for two other of Lou's compositions. Several major international vocal groups have recorded Lou's mass.

The St. Cecilia Soc. sang a traditional Latin Requiem at the wake of Lou's partner Bill Colvig. We informally sang the Requiem for friends and people we admire who have passed, most recently for Aretha. Friend Teresa Ellis paid a modest fee to do a Requiem for Arthur, her cat. At the Santa Cruz Museum of Art & History in 2012, as an event for the ESPRESSO POLICE/Caffe Pergolesi, the Early Years 1974-77 exhibition, we sang a traditional Requiem Mass for departed Caffe workers, customers and Penny University founders and patrons: Tony Gallagher, Chris Hartnack, Elaine Heuman, Lou Harrison & Bill Colvig, Ann Cochrane, Ed Carrillo, Mary Comstock, Hal Painter, Gene Lewis, Tom Scribner, Brian Strong, Pat Liteky, Gary Garman, Candy Counerty, Ros Day, Michaelangelo Rosato, Charlie & Bob Hall, Page & Eloise Smith, Mary Holmes, Sara Boutelle, Donald Nicholl, Betty Caffe Latte and many others.

Only once did we, Julie, Karen Smith, Judy and Frank, perform Peking Opera, but nobody noticed. Our abbreviated version of Lady White Snake, in English, with gongs, cymbals and wood block made no obvious impression on the early morning Caffe patrons.

We have added Georgian and Balkan music, thanks to Mark Forry, to our formerly limited repertoire of dozens of Latin masses. We also, on special occasions, sing our rendition of Blue Velvet, as well as plenty of traditional Christmas carols at our secular Xmas party.

The St. Cecilia Society sang the Requiem for the closing of the fifth or sixth iteration of the Caffe Pergolesi in September 2017. The only resemblance to the original Caffe, other than the name, was the ceiling mural painted by Ann Cochrane.

Art

We preferred the pristine brick walls over the run of the mill coffee house art. Many artists, mostly students, badgered us to show their work. The only painting in the place was a copy of The Wedding of Cana by Paolo Veronese gifted by our friend Bob Ludlow. It was placed high above the entrance door. We admired Futzie Nutzle's elegantly simple/complex, often witty, drawings. He was the only artist to have an exhibition in the Caffe while we owned it. Nutzle also made a Caffe menu.

Our late night hijinx passed for what some call art,. I call it performance art.

Newspapers on library rods were located on the walls behind the pews. We subscribed to the Manchester Guardian, Pravda, and frequently had copies of Trailer Park News, Police Gazette, The Catholic Worker, La Monde, La Stampa, Corriere della Sera. Most were out of date, save those to which we subscribed.

Julie Marlow reports: "We sometimes fenced with the newspaper sticks before closing."

Nutzle, Dan Landry and spouses joined us for a field trip to a restaurant trade show in San Francisco. We dressed in costumes we thought representative of what sleazy fast food owners might wear. I wore white shoes, a gold chain, sunglasses and some other outlandish clothing.

We were reluctant to have a tip jar, but the staff felt it necessary. Hence, the Cinzano Brothers Defense Fund label on the jar. We all made up fantastic stories about the brothers for our own amusement. We would sometimes keep a bottle of Cinzano behind the counter to fortify ourselves.

Employment Test and Employees

Originally, we thought Judy, Lynn, Jack Crick and I could run the place with a little help from Judy's brother Chris and Don Day. How naive we were. Soon we were hiring friends of friends and good customers.

Nearly every day many applicants pleaded for a job at the Caffe. My attempt to counter this was a three page mimeographed test constructed by Judy and me. It was silly, yet got to the point of discouraging those who would not fit our conception of the perfect espresso jerk.

Some questions from the test might give a hint of what the Caffe was about:

True or False —

2. The Caffe Pergolesi was created so that the boss and her husband would get rich.

3. All music is appropriate for the Caffe.

5. The unadorned brick walls of the Caffe await a Michelangelo.

7. Punctuality, cleanliness and piety are desirable traits for an employee.

8. As an employee of the Caffe you will submit to all manner of humiliations.

20. While flirting with customers, an employee will wash dishes or be productive in some manner.

Some other questions: Multiple choice

23. Which of the following types of music is not suitable for the Caffe?

a. Peking Opera. b. Gagaku. c. Bluegrass. d. Singing whales. e. Blues.

26. Which of the following books is not on the Caffe required reading list?

a) Dice Man; b) The Circus of Dr. Lao; c) Lore of the Chinese Lute; d) War of the Gurus; e) Puckoon; f) Rubyfruit Jungle; g) Trailer Camp Woman; h). Pyramid Power.

Essay questions:

31. Is there any task too demeaning for your status or self-respect? What and Why?

32. Could you spend your entire shift listening to Gregorian chant and Mozart? Explain why or why not.

Joe Schultz, of India Joze fame, was the only person to get a perfect score on the test. He baked Bundt cake for us and was an espresso jerk extraordinaire.

The Caffe was open from 7 AM to midnight, and closing at 1 AM on Fridays and Saturdays. From the opening day we always were busy. Over fifty people worked at the Caffe during the slightly more than three years we owned it. Seventeen were on the staff near the end, with two or three workers needed on each shift. All were well educated, artists, writers, musicians, filmmakers, chefs, a sex worker or two, carpenters, dancers, theater folk, and even a few academics. I don't recall if we hired any surfers. Nearly all of the expresso jerks became good friends, with several who are now my closest confidants.

Initially, Judy and I trained and supervised new workers. Dan Landry, Victor Schiffrin and Doug Montalbano, as sometime managers, were also competent teachers. All too often we had to retrain some of the workers, especially those who ignored the Caffe memos. A sloppy caffe latte was not tolerated. A watery espresso was a cardinal sin. Spending ten minutes washing a spoon was not acceptable, even if stoned. All espresso jerks trained by Judy and Frank are card carrying officers in the ESPRESSO POLICE, yet another Foreman art project.

We took several of the staff on a field trip to the Caffe Trieste to see how a real caffe worked. Then to Vanessi's restaurant, where we sat at the counter to see how things are done correctly.

Barbara Weisman on Dope

Lisa liked working shifts with me for probably only one reason. She would grab me and take me off and insist I get stoned with her beforehand, which I never learned to refuse. Then, though, I would become exceptionally self-conscious and unable to work the counter: I would bury myself in the dishes, looking no one in the face. I am sure this suited her fine: a whole shift without dishwashing.

Memos

Addressed to staff, or stuffs given Frank's unreadable hand, the memos indicate our struggle with learning to be bosses with workers who were our friends. Craig Johnson told me recently that Judy was the best boss he has had in nearly fifty years of employment. How to make a business work smoothly, when run by a distracted artist married to a compulsive one, was evident in the sheer number of memos. There were six number 6 memos. Given there were 17 employees and not all could make the staff meetings in the hot tub, I began writing memos to express our concerns. Judy, Doug and Julie also wrote memos, often attempting to explain my oblique and often convoluted suggestions. Making a weekly schedule was the most daunting task Judy dealt with and Doug tried too, but he gave up in frustration. Seventeen espresso jerks of varying skills, attention spans, personality quirks and altered states of consciousness, who all had preferences for one of the three daily shifts, and which of the others they would, or would not like be scheduled to work with, made this task all but were impossible. Hence, seven memos were written concerning the schedule, to no avail. We were good guys, attempting to be fair and conciliatory, but not particularly efficient bosses. My Mediterranean temper was best served by writing memos, many of which were composed in drunken or stoned states of anger, hope and frustration at trying to run a business.

   Memo #34: If you are behind the counter, you are working.

   Memo #27: No smoking behind the counter, or inside the Caffe. This means you Dan. (As anti-smoking advocates, we were the first retail food related business with a non-smoking policy in Santa Cruz.)

   Memo #4 The answer appears to be in the dice. THE DICEMAN is required reading. (For a few weeks The Diceman was number three best seller in Santa Cruz, thanks to the manipulation of Bookshop Santa Cruz staff.)

   Memo #3: The customer is seldom right.

   Memo #6: Wash the glasses clean.

   Memo #9: Prices. Get with the times. We live in a capitalist system. Our prices are fair. We serve high quality, well prepared food and drinks. Be not apologetic about our prices. One need only drive to Capitola for higher prices and lower quality. Inflation has caused everything to increase in price.

Also, remember the Caffe is a business, not a social service agency. If you feel guilty about our prices, keep it to yourself or ask us for an explanation. Don't forget sales tax is included. The Caffe Trieste charges 55 cents for espresso.

Memo #43: Please read and obey all memos.

Memo #85: Who gets free coffee explicated in detail. Nutzle free everything forever. Free everything for staff while working. Don Day free everything because he invested in the Caffe, Lynn too. Off duty staff are entitled to free coffee or tea. Significant others of staff get free drinks if, like Teresa, they help bus the tables. Musicians free everything while playing.Bob Hall free coffee. Billy Allen free coffee to sober him up. That's that.

Memo #17: My memo on our music policy ran for three pages explicitly pointing out that the Caffe was not named Pergolesi for nothing. I suggested searching of our Caffe Pergolesi sign, if in doubt.

Memo #12: Breaks. What can be said? It distresses us to come to the Caffe only to find customers waiting in line, dishes on tables and only one person at work. Check out the Caffe Trieste.

Memo #13: The Caffe is not a health food joint.

Memo #47: Surliness. Be selective. Don't put your shit on customers just because you don't have to take any. We find downright rudeness difficult to explain.

Memo #6: Morning shift cleans the bathroom clean in the bookshop.

Julie Marlow comments on the bathroom we shared with the bookshop: "Barbara, Roxanne and I papered the bookshop bathroom with pages from Gravity's Rainbow."

Naturally, many of the memos were annotated with wise-ass staff comments. Some were helpful and often witty, especially those by Hal Painter and Doug Montalbano . Lisa Emmons had the foresight to save many of the memos. Why I am not sure, but we were happy she did. Thank you Lisa.

Attmosphere, Feeling, Ambience, Vibe

What was the Caffe really like? The times were fertile, open, experimental and good fun. We were lucky to have been around Santa Cruz and San Francisco in the Sixties and early Seventies. We were aware that these were special times with important changes happening. There were fewer people and cars then which made existence a little friendlier. Also, fewer down and out folk eased operating a business. We took care of a regular customer in an orange jump suit who seemed over the top crazy, but he bothered nobody. When he got too weird, we asked him to leave. He did so without question. We also took care of a couple of drunks. Billy Allen was the most notorious, but he drank his coffee and left without complaint. And then there were those who stole cups and sugar. We simply confronted them and asked they refrain from doing so, and not to come back. Not once did we call the police.

You had to have been there to get it. Much of what went on was memorable, if ephemeral, and doesn't lend itself to written accounts. Those of us who were in and around the Caffe between the summer of 1973 and June of 1977 have memories worth sharing. My recollections are clear and accurate, or so I thought until hearing and reading the accounts of others who were there then. My memory is somewhat clouded and perhaps I was too intimately involved to be accurate. Until April 26, 2015, I had Judy, my wife of fifty-four years, to keep my recollections honest. She was my partner in crime — we both spent a day in jail in 1968 for painting a large mural on Kearny St. at Broadway, with several friends, two of whom later became affiliated with the Caffe. Judy's perfect Dada attitude added subtle wit to all we did. Now, without Judy, I have my friends who worked at the Caffe with whom I check my perceptions. I somewhat randomly include observations by people connected with the Caffe. Often their recollections differ, and even contradict, mine. An example of this is in Gary Patton's thank you letter.

Memories of the early years, 1974-77
by Gary A. Patton, November 15, 1990

I was first elected to the Santa Cruz County board of Supervisors in November 1974. Shortly after taking office in January 1975, I began a series of Monday morning meetings at the Caffe Pergolesi. These meetings were intended to inform constituents about upcoming matters on the Agenda, and to let local citizens have direct access to their County Supervisor. Nowadays, all members of the Board of Supervisors hold similar meetings but in 1975, this was an innovation.

For almost sixteen years, I hosted these meetings at the Caffe Pergolesi — later renamed Cafe Zinho — each Monday morning preceding a Board meeting. My last meeting was on October 16, 1989, the day before the Loma Prieta Earthquake, which destroyed this beautiful and significant spot forever.

What most remains in my mind about the Caffe Pergolesi is a vision of the physical space itself. That memoranda a memory of the activities it always contained. This cubic brick coffee house was like a "nuclear reactor for ideas," containing within its relatively small confines great controversies, discussions, jokes, performances, political strategy session, Gregorian chants, and the Penny University!

Art exhibits always graced the walls at the Caffe Pergolesi, and all of one's senses were put into play....

No other place has ever been — or ever will be — quite like the Caffe Pergolesi. It was a unique combination of bricks, mortar, and the human spirit, and was truly at the very "heart" of Santa Cruz. I mourn its passing — and celebrate its unperishing contributions.

This is an instance where Gary was wrong. Only once in the early years were art works displayed on the Caffe walls — Futzie Nutzle's ink drawings were up for two months December 1974 through January 1975, or maybe it was 1975/6. Perhaps Gary saw some so-called art in a later version of the Caffe.

I vaguely remember that Gary's predecessor County Supervisor Pat Litkey held a few meetings at the Caffe, and subsequently he gave occasional poetry readings there.

Bob Hall

The Caffe was also the place where members of the Downtown C. Of C, (not affiliated with the Greater S.C.C. of C.) organized to : defend Spring Fair artists, craftspersons and street performers from the crackdown of the Downtown Assn. and a conservative City Council of that time.

Never in my wildest nightmare did I ever expect to be a founding member of the Chamber of Commerce, even one that shared some of my values.

And then there is expresso etc.

A good strong espresso was our signature drink. A tasty simple shot, like those readily available anywhere in Italy, is what we aimed for. We served variations of espresso - cappuccino, caffe latte, as well as teas, hot chocolate and pastries. We also offered simple lunch items — dolmas, bagel & cream cheese, etc.

Janet Ing Freeman

I have sometimes been successful in restraining myself from telling a total stranger in some lesser cafe how to foam milk, but at other moments I have not been able to withhold the vital information 'it's all in the sound'.

We had hoped the espresso jerks would get it together to form a co-op to buy the Caffe. They did not. Shortly after selling the Caffe, the workers formed the Espresso Workers United, affiliated with AFL/CIO, in reaction to the new owners sloppy management.

After selling the Caffe we created the ESPRESSO POLICE in order to continue our efforts to spread the word about good espresso around the world, especially in Santa Cruz. We have either failed, or have much work ahead of us.

Futzie Nutzle:
Drawings for Caffe Pergolesi, 1970s

COFFEE ~ COFFEE

ESPRESSO ~ If you don't know what it is you don't want it.
40¢

ESPRESSO ROMANO ~ Demitasse of ESPRESSO Coffee w/ twist of LEMON PEEL: tart and SATISFYING, austere.
40¢

ESPRESSO MACCHIATO ~ Demitasse of ESPRESSO Coffee w/ a spot of STEAMED MILK
45¢

ESPRESSO CON PANA ~ Demitasse of ESPRESSO Coffee w/ WHIPPED CREAM.
50¢

DOUBLE ESPRESSO ~ A cup nearly full of ESPRESSO. ~ NO steamed MILK.
50¢

CAPPUCINO ~ ESPRESSO, in a 6 oz. CUP, topped with STEAMED MILK: RICH CREAMY & RIGHT
60¢

CAPPUCINO GRANDE ~ DOUBLE ESPRESSO in a 9 oz. cup, topped with STEAMED MILK: for HABITUEES.
70¢

CAFFE VALENCIA ~ DOUBLE ESPRESSO in a 6 oz. cup topped with whipped cream, orange bits, & a half oz. of orange syrup.
70¢

CAFFE LATTÉ ~ 10 oz. glass of STEAMED MILK with ESPRESSO: MELLOW, BUT a touch of piquancy.
65¢

ESPRESSO MOCHA ~ DUTCH cocoa and ESPRESSO, with STEAMED MILK, topped of course, with whipped cream.
80¢

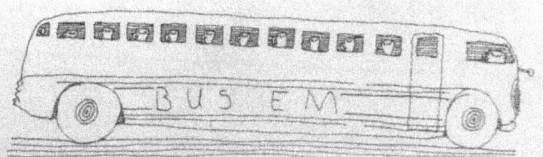

Chapter 12: Lynda Francis May
Butterfly Productions

I arrived in Santa Cruz in January 1975 and shortly thereafter met Elizabeth Gips. She was a "free spirit" living in her van with her dog, traveling around, and producing radio shows. Later on, she produced "Changes" radio show on KZSC and KKUP interviewing a wide range of prominent personalities. She seemed to know everything and everyone. After all, she had lived on Love Street in Haight-Ashbury and the Doors had written a song about her. She and a few other people would come over to a house Peter Stafford and I shared in Live Oak and we would muse about the future. We were S.M.I.L.E. advocates. Tim Leary described SMILE as Space Migration, Higher Intelligence and Life Extension. This small group of futurists actually brought a number of people, like Dr. Bronner and Jacques Valle, to Santa Cruz over the years to enlighten us on various topics. We called ourselves the Linkage group, linking art, science and mysticism. The group grew in size and people like Tom Fitzwater — artist, Earle Lane — Kirlian photographer, and Bruce Eisner — journalist and later author of MDMA, and others joined us.

In the next two years, events moved quickly. Peter was writing the Psychedelics Encyclopedia and I was helping. We'd go up to San Francisco to the Fitz Hugh Ludlow Library monthly and Peter would read all the books they had on a given subject. He would synthesize the material in his head and then would tell me what he had learned. We recorded the info; I would type it up on a manual typewriter and he would edit it. I would type it up again and organize the information. While working on the book, we conceived our son on July 14 (Bastille Day) on acid and he was born in 1977. Later that year, Psychedelics Encyclopedia was published.

1977 was a fruitful year and the book coming out energized Linkage. We planned to have a reception to celebrate at UCSC in October. We decided to invite many famous people at their own expense and on short notice and people like Ram Dass, Leary, and Metzner all said yes. We contacted Dr. Albert Hofmann, discover of LSD 25, in Switzerland and he agreed to attend as well. This was his first trip to America and we were stoked. So were the 3,000 people who attended what became known as Colloquium I — LSD A Generation Later. Colloquium II — The Future of Consciousness followed in 1981 and the Bridge Conference at Stanford in 1991. We set the standard for "New Age" gatherings with the format we used copied for years.

The news of Colloquium I reached Woodstock N.Y. where Nina Graboi was living at the time. Nina had been very active in the formative years of Millbrook and the League for Spiritual Discovery in Manhattan. She had missed the opportunity to join us at the first Colloquium, but made it out to visit us the next year. Things had quieted down in Woodstock and she had accurately ascertained that Santa Cruz was "where it was happening." Nina had grown up Jewish in Vienna and had to flee Hitler's grasp. She fled Vienna as an aristocrat and landed in England as a nanny. Her sophistication and spiritual awakenings were a great fit for Santa Cruz and she had a ready-made community. Within a short time after visiting, she moved to Santa Cruz. Her deep connections to the luminaries of the day, like Prem Das and Lama Ole Nydahl, were an essential component to making Colloquium II a success. With Nina's direction, we held "Salons" and delved into topics of interest to us. The Linkage group transformed itself into the Psychedelic Education Center. The P.E.C. produced the Blotter newspaper and magazine. Over a decade or so, Blotter became Island Views, after Huxley's novel Island. Stafford, Eisner and others formed the Island Group, which eventually spun off a radical element called the F.O.G. group — the Formless Ocean Group. The F.O.G. group had Physicist Nick Herbert and Robert Anton Wilson as special participants.

After Colloquium II, Nina Graboi, Elizabeth Gips and I realized Santa Cruz was fertile ground for all the ideas coming out of the Colloquia and realized that many of these people were journeying down to Esalen from the Bay area on a regular basis. We thought we could continue to educate the public by "heading our friends off at the pass" and waylaying them for a night in Santa Cruz. After much discussion, the three of us formed Butterfly Productions. Nina's natural affinity for children benefitted my family a lot. I thought of her as my spiritual mother. We would meet at her house and she always gave my son, Sasha, an iron to play with. She would tell him to pretend it was a train. He spent the time we were talking, taking his train around to many different stations and thoroughly enjoying himself.

Nina's connection to Tim Leary made him a regular for us. We usually asked our guests to give an introductory lecture on Friday evening and then a workshop on Saturday. This became a popular format. Tim was enthusiastically received in Santa Cruz and we usually used Heartwood Spa (now Five Branches) for the daytime events. At times, different people would join us like Robert Dilts, software developer for NLP, and Professor Frank Barron from UCSC. One time we got wind that a group of MADD protesters were going to disrupt our event. We quickly called Tim to cancel, but he objected saying he could not ask for better publicity! We continued Butterfly Productions for a few years, but philosophical differences between Nina and Elizabeth made agreement difficult and after expenses, we had little to show for our efforts, not that we were expecting much. Nina connected with Ralph Abraham and started to help him with various projects.

Elizabeth, Melody Record, and I started Prism Productions, "Reflecting the Light." Our first effort to bring Andy Weil to Santa Cruz to talk about the benefits of Coca leaves flopped. He was unknown then and we lost money. We produced a few more workshops. Nina was always our special guest and we consulted with her regularly.

After a while, I went out on my own starting in 1985 with Perfect Worlds Productions and continued until 1992 supplementing my daytime income a little. Perfect Worlds brought Terence McKenna, Dennis McKenna, Paul Williams, Yasos, Robert Anton Wilson, John Lilly, Kayendres (Mohawk MedicineWoman), Nicki Scully, Ralph Abraham, Stephen Gaskin, Jaron Lanier, and others to share their wisdom with the community. We also held a benefit for the Huichol Indians. We were deeply committed to creating educational events, to sharing information, and to raising awareness. Money was never a motivation, only a consideration. All told, we had a good run!

Chapter 13: Don Monkerud
Elizabeth Gips: The Quintessential Hippy

Ever heard a hippy church on the air? Anyone who listened to KZSC or KKUP in the 1970s through 2000 heard Elizabeth Gips interview a series of spiritual and mental health advocates, innovators, and thinkers. She was a strong-willed woman who wasn't content with convention, superficiality or bombast. Elizabeth probed deeply into human consciousness, seeking answers to perplexing eternal questions of the spirit and human well-being.

I didn't know Elizabeth well when I entered her backyard to conduct an afternoon interview at her house on Union Street at the end of the millennium. I listened to her radio program, "Changes," and was astonished by the various beliefs people held. She and I had a number of things in common: We'd both dropped acid, lived in communes and came to Santa Cruz around the same time. A small energetic woman with a light in her eyes, she seemed to delight in the world and wanted to know more about the world and its people.

Birds flitted between branches, Tibetan prayer flags flapped in the breeze, and a Buddha peeked out from flowers in the peaceful garden. Over two decades older, she was the 40-year-old that my generation didn't trust when we were 20. Was I in for a surprise!

Elizabeth told me her life could have taken a different turn. "I was born on LSD," Elizabeth said. "I'm so grateful that in my middle age I was given that opportunity. Although I didn't, I could have lived my whole life being as a middleclass housewife. In 1966 I dropped acid, experienced God and was able to integrate [that experience] into my life."

Born in 1922 and growing up in Westchester County, N.Y., Elizabeth attended Mills College after her father's death and her family's subsequent move to California. She was unhappy with the very protective and conservative nature of Mills College and planned to transfer to Reed College in Oregon. Instead she married Paul Lansman, a Ph. D. in physics who was ten years her senior, and moved to Saint Louis where she had two children. The creative bohemian community they discovered owned a solid block of old buildings in the center of town, published an avant-garde journal called Neurotica, and held "alcohol parties where marijuana was smoked," and where "mate-swapping was a frequent practice," according to her niece Judith Gips. While in St. Louis she started two import businesses to sell Indian and Chinese clothing and jewelry, but she was ahead of her time — only beatniks bought Asian imports in the 1950s.

After Elizabeth and Paul divorced in the late 1950s, she moved to California to be near her mother and brother who lived there. The mid-1960s found her back importing antiques and jewelry in the Bay Area, selling her wares through Cost Plus Imports. Her business was successful with 52 employees, and grossed half a million dollars in sales her last year. She opened a jewelry store and bought a mansion on Ashbury near the intersection with Haight.

She married for a second time to Dean Wallace, an arts critic for the San Francisco Call-Bulletin and later the San Francisco Chronicle. Dean offered her first LSD and the two of them began attending the Monday Night Classes at San Francisco State led by Stephen Gaskin. Elizabeth began opposing the Vietnam War and opened her house on Ashbury to Vietnam War protestors. Visitors to her house could expect to find books on The Tao Te Ching and The Tibetan Book of the Dead.

Elizabeth was never what the media called "a dirty hippy." Judith Gips said her aunt enjoyed cooking and cleaning and creating a home, even if it was unconventional. Elizabeth often became angry when the kitchen was left a mess, the trash wasn't recycled properly or the meditation room was not set back in order.

"After dropping acid," she told David Jay Brown in his two volume work Mavericks of the Mind, "I walked out of everything — my marriage, my business, my whole life. I took all my clothes and jewelry and dumped them then in the middle of the floor and said, 'everybody dig in — I'm gone.'"

She describes herself in that period as being "messianic," and wanting to turn everyone on, much like many of us when we first smoked marijuana. The way to enlightenment was through psychedelics. She wore her hair long, adopted an elk skin dress, and regarded herself as "too outrageous for society." The fact that the rest of society didn't catch up and remained locked in conventional 1950s styles and thoughts disappointed her. She said people were "afraid to get high."

Her niece Judith Gips recalls, "Elizabeth was something of a 'commuter hippie' traveling back and forth between San Francisco, Nevada City's Seventh Angel Commune, and Los Angeles at various communal houses." Back in San Francisco, Elizabeth became a devoted student of Stephen Gaskin, whom she saw as "the avatar of the Aquarian Age." Judith Gips recalls Elizabeth's deep faith in Stephen's "true vision of the Universe" letters to herself and "whoever else would listen."

In late 1969, Elizabeth purchased a Cadillac Camper parked with a For Sale sign on the street in San Francisco with what little money she had left from giving all her possessions away. She joined Stephen and his four-marriage family in The Caravan, a collection of 200 people traveling across the country in school buses and other live-in vehicles. She settled down with the fledgling idealistic community, The Farm in rural Tennessee, but only lasted seven months. "Power trips," strong egos, poverty and the lack of democracy weren't her idea of communal living.

In December 1971, she left The Farm and visited her brother's family in Los Angeles, where she joined former Farm residents gleaning orchards in Southern California. After returning to San Francisco, she found herself "walking around San Francisco crying hysterically." At the time her mother thought her daughter was "heading for the looney bin," and Elizabeth told Judith Gips that "guru withdrawal is a terrible thing — I felt I was truly psychotic."

She had no idea what to do and decided to return to The Farm. On her way, she visited her son Jeremy in St. Louis, where he had a communal radio station, KDNA (as in deoxyribonucleic acid). This new means of communication enamored her and she began to learn about creative, community-involved radio. After her son sold the station, Elizabeth returned to Missouri and the Ozarks briefly, remarried, also briefly, and traveled back to California where she lived in Santa Barbara. There she arranged a community center which freely distributed donated clothing, food, massages, and workshops on spiritual matters. On a trip to visit her son Jeremy, who was beginning an avant garde country-rock progressive radio station, KFAT, near Gilroy, CA, she decided to settle in Santa Cruz, which would be her home for the remaining years of her life.

"On the other side of Santa Cruz is the Pacific Ocean, and you can't go any farther," Elizabeth said. "There were lots of beach towns on the California coast where all the dissidents went as far as they could in their wanderings. There was already a tolerance for difference, more here than other places. Just look at the way people dress, it reflects a qualitatively different 'head space.'"

"The earth is an insane asylum for all the troubled souls

in the universe," she added. "It gave us this beautiful place and said, 'get yourself well.' Santa Cruz is a place where there's more acceptance of difference, so you aren't tagged or identified as a patient right away. Evolution is learning how to redirect the electrical and chemical reactions in the brain away from fear — that's it, the whole thing. I haven't found it easy and have never met anyone who has done it completely."

The Santa Cruz vibe welcomed Elizabeth. She walked the streets barefoot, smoked a joint, and danced freely. In the early 1970s, people gathered for music at the Cooper House and she, along with the many others on Pacific Avenue, delighted in the public openness. Living was easy as she spent her time on the streets and slept in a turquoise van with yellow trim. Ginger, known as "Rainbow Lady," danced on the street in front of the Cooper House as crowds listened to the band "Warmth" play. She adopted rainbow colored clothing and joined the revelry.

Elizabeth began working at KZSC, where she sometimes slept on the floor. She cooked turkeys and hosted Easter parties, "I invited the street people to come up and play their music, recite their poems and say what they needed to say," she said. Many great musicians, including Lacy J. Dalton and Bob Brozman, played on her show and she gave them plenty of encouragement.

Laura Ellen Hooper, her son Jeremy's partner for many years and the mother of her granddaughter, was then at KKUP (and later at KPIG), called Elizabeth and asked her to do a shift at KKUP. "I started doing three shifts a week — 12 hours on the air, Elizabeth recalled. "I moved out of my house into a van and used KZSC as my home for a while. At least I could go on the air and say what I thought."

On her show "Eclectic Mania," she played a wide assortment of music, based on the theory that if people listened to a type of music they didn't like long enough, they'd grow to like it. She kept the music changing: She played rock, classical, folk and any music she considered "enlightening." You have to remember that even reggae was unpopular among some at the time.

At KZSC, she began "a hippy church on the air," "Changes," which played on Sunday from 10 to 2. The focus was spirituality — one quite different from that found in traditional churches. "It always seemed to me," she said, "that one of the problems of the human race is that we enjoy whipping ourselves about some terrible thing or other that might happen: There's no ozone, no water, too much violence. In my tiny way, I wanted to be an antidote."

In her obituary, which she wrote herself, Elizabeth said "Changes" was "based on the premise that the human race has the capacity to learn compassion." Her own life included a struggle to learn compassion with herself and with others. My impression was that as she grew older she stopped being aggressive in her pursuit of change. Some saw her as "authoritative and bullying" because she offered her opinions freely and wasn't afraid to say what she thought. As she grew older, her approach more and more involved taking people by the hand as if she was showing off a garden, and saying, "look at this, or consider that," rather than making pronouncements. Her approach evolved toward enthralling people and wooing them.

At first, she surprised herself by expressing her own ideas on the radio. She didn't realize that she had something to say when she was younger. Trained to be an aggressive interviewer, Elizabeth threw verbal darts at people until they squirmed and revealed a deeper truth. "My job is unpeeling layers of a person until we get to the kernel of who they are." She wanted to know what was unique about them, what they were at their center. As time went on, she felt her interviews improved because she cared deeply, and she listened closely to what they had to say, a quality she found lacking in many other interviewers. As she aged, she claimed she also "became nicer to people."

Over the course of her lively radio shows, she estimates she conducted 600 to 700 interviews of people on political and spiritual subjects. Her interviewees ranged from leaders to followers, and from ordinary people to the famous, including Nobel prize winners. Her style developed; she asked difficult questions, read passages from books, speeches, and interviews, and delivered her own sometimes rambling spiritual views, mixed with music and her own poetry. What seemed to others as disconnected subjects cohered into a solid point of view. Her shows ran four hours. "Assuming there's a bell curve of consciousness, some listeners were way behind the curve, but most of them were in the ball game. A few were out front, growing consciousness."

A number of her interviewees were spiritual, by which she meant teachers with a capital T. Some were enamored with themselves, self-important or too serious. Others she described as "small t" teachers, by which she meant, "It's nice if you can laugh at yourself and most people have a hard time with that."

Some of her interviewees included such people as: Dr. Ralph Abraham, world famous authority on the science and mathematics of Chaos Theory; John Anderson, lead singer for "Yes" and a spiritual leader; Woableza Dakota, a Dakota/Lakota storyteller who collected stories from North and South American indigenous communities; singer/songwriter Karen Stern, president of the South Bay Astrological Society; David Jay Brown, a local author who wrote 16 books on the evolution of consciousness; Daniel Siebert, an ethnobotanist researching Salvia divinorum; Dr. David Morehouse, a veteran of the US military's remote viewing program, who wrote, Nonlethal Weapons: War Without Death; Cheryl Magrill, co-founder of a group trying to stop Low-Frequency Active Sonar, which has detrimental effects on whales and dolphins; and Marge Cuddeback, who teaches seminars on developing intuitive gifts, chakra, healing, and hypnotic regression.

The tag line for Elizabeth's Exploration in Consciousness include such subjects as: Shamanism, Buddhism, Philosophy, Mind-Body Research, Indigenous Elders, Mysticism, Ecstasy, Wisdom, Prophesy, Altered States, Psychedelics, Insight, Healing, Entheogens, Environmental Stewardship, Social Justice and Global Transformation. If you lived in Santa Cruz during the 25 years of her radio programs, no doubt you've heard some of these shows. There was a large community devoted to following such subjects.

Elizabeth recommended to me her 1995 book, The Scrapbook of a Haight Ashbury Pilgrim: Spirit, Sacraments, & Sex in 1967-68, a unique and honest collection of her poetry, drawings, and musings about living in the Haight. Particularly amusing today is her glossary of Haight-Ashbury-ese, in which she defines such words as acid, Hippy Hill, hanging out, head, munchies, bum trip and white light. I imagine that such books will become symbolic of the age and will be referred to in the future in scholarly works.

Far from being stuck with an intellectual viewpoint, she practiced meditation, and yoga, and supported a number of activist projects, including the Homeless Garden Project, the Resource Center for Non-violence, Wo/Men's alliance for Medical Marijuana or WAMM, The Holy Hemp Sisters, and other activist groups.

Throughout my interview with Elizabeth, Paddy Long, her

mate of 17 years, listened attentively, adding comments and prompts where helpful. Relationships with men weren't always easy for Elizabeth, who was married three times, and she told her niece Judith that being with Paddy was "the first really sane sexual relationship I was ever in."

Between marriages, she spent many years alone. "I used to do yoga by the light house or at the beach every morning rain or shine, and I prayed to the Goddesses to teach me never to fall in love again," she said. "Instead of 'falling in love,' I realized that being able to love was an enormous gift. It was a present in my old age. It's wonderful."

Paddy was one of the organizers of the Spiritual Emergency Network, which he referred to as SIN, with a hearty laugh. When they first met, Paddy had several disagreements with Elizabeth and came to discuss them over dinner. He never left. From New York and ordained as a Marist Brother, Paddy had a doctorate in history, a masters in counseling, a year working with the Dakota/Lakota nation, and also worked at Esalen Institute with Stanislav Grof, MD, who studied consciousness for 60 years. Paddy reminded me of a bearded Irish Catholic priest without the rosary. He cared deeply for the homeless, handed out blankets, and checked on those reduced to sleeping on the streets. He was a vociferous critic of Santa Cruz's ban on public sleeping.

Paddy recounted a recent encounter he had on SIN's Suicide Prevention Line. I can't recall whether he actually went there, but he received a call from a woman in a motel. She was distraught and wanted to kill herself after she had sex with a friend — the devil came out of his body and entered hers. Paddy asked if she had a spiritual belief and she replied she'd grown up a Southern Baptist. Paddy asked if they could pray together.

As they prayed, housekeeping began knocking on the

door. The woman's reservation was over and she had to leave. Housecleaning needs to clean the room, the maid warned. They began praying again. The knock on the door came again, "You have to leave!"

"Please wait, we're almost through," Paddy pleaded. After being interrupted several times by housekeeping and more knocking on the door, Paddy helped the woman free herself from the devil and leave the room. While he took the woman's plight seriously, he found the whole episode amusing due to the interruptions from housekeeping.

It was evident that Paddy cared deeply for Elizabeth and the two delighted in each other's company. He died within weeks of her death at the age of 79, in June of 2001. Before her death from pulmonary disease caused by a long-time tobacco habit, Elizabeth told Eric Meece of Metro that service was the key element to a contented and happy life. "My spiritual life started with that LSD trip," she said, "but I don't think you need psychedelics. Once you get that [spiritual awakening], you have to spend the rest of your life letting other people know how to get that."

(I'd like to thank Marigold Fine, videographer and long-time resident of Lama Foundation, New Mexico; David Jay Brown, a local author who wrote 16 books on the evolution of consciousness; Debra Heavens, a nurse and former resident of The Farm; Tony McGettigan, author of A Voyage in Consciousness, and other titles, and friend of Elizabeth: Palika Benton, friend of Elizabeth and long-time spiritual devotee; and Judith Gips, Elizabeth's niece, professional educator and the person Elizabeth noted in her final papers as her "spiritual heir.")

Chapter 14: Ralph Abraham:
Nina Graboi — A Spiritual Journey

Nina leapt into the future a decade ago, but is still fondly remembered by many of our community. Here is a short story of her journey, extracted from her book, *One Foot in the Future*, of 2000.

Onramp, 1918-1966

Nina was born in Vienna in 1918. Her childhood was wonderful until the rise of Nazism in Austria in 1938.

To escape it, she was sent to London, and then moved on to Belgium in 1939. There she met Mischa/Michel, a 28-year-old Russian emigre. They were married in 1940, and walked to France to escape the German bombs.

After some months of detainment in North Africa, they reached New York in 1941, moved on to California in time for Pearl Harbor, then back to New York in 1942, where they created a successful business. They separated in 1966.

One Foot into the Future, 1966-1979

She opened a lecture bureau. Among her clients were Alan Watts, Paul Krassner, Charles Tart, Peter Stafford, and the multimedia group USCO (including Gerd Stern.)

She met Timothy Leary, Richard Alpert, and Ralph Metzner, and began to go regularly to the mansion in Millbrook. She attended an LSD conference in San Francisco in 1966, along with LSD luminaries such as Allan Ginsburg, Frank Barron, Huston Smith, Paul Lee, and the Grateful Dead.

Returning to New York, she had her first major trip: smoking DET with Ralph Metzner. It was July 27, 1966. A few days later she had her first LSD trip in Millbrook. A new life began.

She moved to an apartment in Greenwich Village, a couple of blocks from where I had lived a few years earlier. She became the founding director of the New York Center for the League of Spiritual Discovery. In 1968 she moved to Woodstock and opened a meditation center. And in 1979 she moved on to Santa Cruz. Her book ended here, where she wrote:

The young girl in Vienna, the refugee, the woman in love, the party-giving Long Island matron, the producer of star-studded plays, the studious inward-looking seeker, the director of the LSD Center and the Woodstock Transformation Center, the shopkeeper and mother-figure to the baby-boomers, the welfare recipient, the baby sitter, the writer. Were all these persons me?

Santa Cruz, 1980-2000

Another LSD conference was organised at UCSC in 1981, and Nina came to Santa Cruz to help with its organisation. Shortly after, she became my personal assistant and close friend. She was a marvelous help with my work, assisting with translations from French and German, managing all the correspondence and filling, and so on.

In June of 1996 I was invited to a conference in Vienna. I knew that Nina had been longing for a visit to her childhood home, and approaching her 80th birthday, this could be a good time.

So I brought her with me to the conference, and we walked for hours around Vienna, where she showed me her home, schools, friends' homes, the park where her father took her as a child, and so on.

It was said the antisemitism in Vienna was a thing of the past, but with her fluency in the local vernacular, she found that to be untrue. In fact, when we went to a synagogue for services, we found armed guards outside as there had been recent attacks.

The leap into the future

Nina passed in her bed at home after a short illness. The friends who discovered her body reported that she looked happy, and was poised for a leap into the next world.

CONCLUSION

In the Conclusion of the first volume of this series, I wrote:

I began the Hip Santa Cruz History Project and website with the idea that the 1960s Hip Culture movement was a miracle.

At the end of the second volume I wrote:

The story emerging in this volume continues the story of this miraculous transformation ...

And in closing the third volume I assigned credit for this miracle to the psychedelic revolution.

Ending this fourth volume I can admit that there were multiple factors in the evolution of Hip, not only LSD. In the further development of the various threads emerging from the miraculous 1960s, as documented in this volume, the beat goes on in an entangled complex system of mutual synergy.

There is no end to miracles.

Index

Symbols

25th Century Ensemble 22, 26

A

Acid Test 35, 36
Alan Watts 180
Albert Hofmann 167
Al DiLudovico 57
Allan Ginsburg 180
Al van Zyl 57
American Friends Service Committee 95, 96, 97
Annie Steinhart 60

B

Baba Ram Das 64
Balloon Newspaper 25
Barn 50, 52, 56, 57
Beatles 62
Be Here Now 64
Black Panthers 113
Blaine House Studs 121
Bob Brozman 174
Bob Dylan 64
Bob Hall 143, 145, 149, 151, 157, 160
Bookshop Santa Cruz 84, 136, 145, 156
Brothers Karamosov 84
Bruce Eisner 166
Bruce Kleinsmith 25
Butterfly Productions 166, 168

C

Cabrillo College 56, 101, 125, 131
Caffe Pergolesi 138, 162
Cannabis Sativa 108, 109, 114, 115, 122
Carmella Weintraub 83
Catalyst 55, 56, 64, 121, 124
Cathy Puccinelli 54

Cecil Williams 72
Chadwick Program 59
Changes 166, 170, 175
Charles Tart 180
Chuck and Esther Abbot 84
City Council 81, 93
City Library 88
Common Ground 73
Community Hospital 127
Community Studies 129, 130
Connoisseur Cannabis 107
Controlled Substances Act 111
Cooper House 83, 84, 86, 174
CORE (Congress of Racial Equality) 72
Costanoan Commons 65
Cowell College 74
Cupola Gallery 24

D

David Jay Brown 172, 176, 179
David Theirmann 95
Dean McHenry 48
Dean Quarnstrom 31
Dennis McKenna 169
Dirty Girls farm 60
Dominican Hospital 24, 25
Don McCaslin 84
Don Monkerud 9, 38, 68, 170
Duke 60

E

Elizabeth Gips 166, 168, 170, 171, 172, 173, 174, 175, 177, 179
Esalen Institute 178

F

Fillmore 62
Fitz Hugh Ludlow Library 166
Frank Barron 168, 180
Frank Foreman 27, 136
Free Spaghetti Dinner 27, 58, 122
Futzie Nutzle 17, 25, 162

G

Gary Patton 159, 160
Gerd Stern 180
Good Fruit Company 99
Good Times 100
Grateful Dead 180
Gregory Bateson 132

H

Haight-Ashbury 166
Haze 114, 115, 116
Heartwood Spa 168
High Times 56
Hip History of Santa Cruz 67, 107
Hip Pocket Bookstore 56
History of Consciousness 131
Holy Hemp Sisters 177
Homeless Garden Project 177
Huey Newton 145
Huston Smith 180
Huxley 168

I

Institute for the Study of Nonviolence 78

J

Jacques Valle 166
James Pike 74, 75, 76
Jami Cassady 10, 50
Joan Baez 64, 71, 78
Joe Lysowski 21
Joe Schultz 154
John Lilly 169
John Tuck 57
Judy Foreman 136

K

Kent State 75
KKUP 166, 170
Korea War 72
KZSC 166, 170, 174

L

Lacy J. Dalton 174
Lama Foundation 179
League of Spiritual Discovery 181
Leon Tabory 51
Leviathan 27
Lighthouse Field 82
Lighthouse Point 85
Logos book store 84
Loma Prieta earthquake 80, 85
Louden Nelson Community Center 124
Lou Harrison 146, 150, 151
LSD 23, 31, 32, 33, 34, 35, 36, 51, 111, 167, 170, 171, 179, 180, 183
LSD conference 180, 181
Lynda Francis May 166

M

Marijuana 107, 108, 109, 110, 111, 112, 117, 121, 171, 172
Mark Primack 87
Martin Luther King 72
Mary Duffield 61
Mary Holmes 9, 38, 39, 48, 151
Mavericks of the Mind 172
Max Hartstein 22, 24
May Diaz 132
MDMA 111, 166
Medical Marijuana 107, 117
Merrill College 104
Merrill Field Program 97
Merry Pranksters 35, 64
Mescaline 111
Metro 27, 179
Mike Corral 117
Mills College 170
Misha B. Adams 118
Moe's Alley 64
Monterey Pop Festival 24
Montessori school 41
Morongo Indian Reservation 96

N

Nancy Tanner 132

Neal Cassady 10, 51
Neal Coonerty 27
Neem Karoli Baba 37
Nick Herbert 168
Nicki Scully 169
Nina Graboi 167, 180
Nonlethal Weapons: War Without Death 177
Nonviolence Center 77
Nuclear-free Santa Cruz County 80
Nuclear Weapons Freeze 68

O

One Foot in the Future 180
Original Haze 114, 115

P

Pacific Garden Mall 84, 85, 122
Paddy Long 177
Page Smith 39, 47, 74, 144, 145, 151
Pat Bisconti 25
Paul Lee 145, 180
Penny University 38, 144, 145, 151, 159
Perfect Worlds Productions 169
Pergolesi coffee shop 84
Peter Beagle 118
Peter Stafford 166, 180
Phil Ochs 18
Pogonip 65, 85
Pot 57, 62
Pranksters 23
Prem Das 167
Prism Productions 169
Psychedelics Encyclopedia 166
Purple Haze 115

R

Ralph Abraham 25, 57, 95, 116, 169, 176, 180
Ralph Metzner 180
Ram Dass 31, 33, 37, 167
Resource Center for Nonviolence 68, 80
Richard Alpert 31, 32, 33, 34, 35, 37, 180
Rick Alan 54, 107

Rick Gladstone 123
Rita Bottoms 27
Robert Anton Wilson 168, 169
Rolling Stones 62, 73
Ron Boise 22
Ron Lau 136

S

Sai Baba 31
Salvia divinorum 177
San Francisco State 171
San Jose State 73, 129, 131
Santa Cruz Cannabis Buyers Club 117
Santa Cruz Midwives' Collective 126
Santa Cruz Resource Center for Nonviolence 78
Santa Cruz Sentinel 127, 129
S.C.A.M.P 27
Scott Kennedy 68
Sharon Lau 136
Silver Haze 115
Snail 124
SNCC 62
Sons of Champlin 124
Special Collections at UCSC 27
Spinny Walker 25
Spiritual Emergency Network (SIN) 178
Stanford 21, 31, 70, 73, 78, 167
Stanislav Grof 178
Stephen Gaskin 169, 171, 172
Sticky Wicket 65
Sundaz! 122, 124
Sundial 18
Susie Cream-cheese 22

T

Teacup Restaurant 84
Terence McKenna 169
Thunder Machine 22
Timothy Leary 34, 166, 167, 168, 180
T. Mike Walker 17
Tom Noddy 85
Tom Scribner 124
Trident Newspaper 62

U

UC Berkeley 72, 73, 96, 97, 132
UC Extension 101
UCLA 46, 47, 101
UC Santa Barbara 76, 96, 137
UC Santa Cruz (UCSC) 27, 38, 39, 48, 73, 77, 97, 101, 102, 112, 121, 124, 125, 128, 130, 131, 132, 136, 150, 167, 168, 181
United Bar 98
Unity Church 87
USCO 180

V

Valerie Corral 117
Vietnam War 66, 72, 74, 171

W

Warmth 174
War on Drugs 108, 109
War Resisters League 80
White Buffalo 27
White Lightning, 36
Wilder Ranch 82, 85
Wobbly Movement 124
Wo/Men's Alliance for Medical Marijuana 117
Woodstock Festival 83
Woodstock West 73

www.ingramcontent.com/pod-product-compliance
Lightning Source LLC
Chambersburg PA
CBHW051929160426
43198CB00012B/2084